Handguns & Rifles

THE FINEST WEAPONS FROM AROUND THE WORLD

Handguns & Rifles

THE FINEST WEAPONS FROM AROUND THE WORLD

IAN HOGG

THE LYONS PRESS

First Lyons Press
edition published in 2003

First produced in 1999 by
PRC Publishing Ltd,
64 Brewery Road, London N7 9NT
A member of **Chrysalis** Books plc

All inquiries should be addressed to:
The Globe Pequot Press,
P.O. box 480, Guilford, CT 06437

The Lyons Press is an imprint of The Globe Pequot Press

The Library of Congress Cataloguing-in-Publication Data is available on file

ISBN 1 58574 835 8

Printed and bound in China

Contents

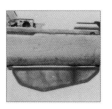

Introduction

Revolvers

Automatic pistols may have changed little over the years, but their promotion and sales material certainly has. This is FN's BDA9 double-action pistol (fires 9x19mm NATO rounds), looking businesslike against a rock and fire background.

The 20th century will probably turn out to have been one of the most violent centuries in history; perhaps the most violent if judged by the number of casualties. Scarcely a day has gone by on which there was not some sort of war, uprising or other lethal disturbance in progress. Because of this the weapon designers and manufacturers have been continuously busy, and charting the path of weapon development and technology through the century is a complex and interesting business. Except for pistols, that is. The history of the pistol throughout this century is a relatively straightforward story, for two basic reasons. Firstly, the revolver had reached its peak of perfection at the turn of the century, and except for a few aberrant models which failed to stay the course, the revolver of the year 2000 is not going to be very much different from that of 1900 — except in material and method of manufacture. Secondly, the number of ways you can make a practical automatic pistol work are limited (principally by the size of the weapon and the need to be able to operate it with one hand) and the variations on the available designs are equally limited.

Having read that, you may well be asking what the rest of the book can possibly be about? But even though the technical advances in the handgun field have not been so spectacular as those in, say, the military rifle or machine gun field, they nevertheless exist and, together with the designs which failed to prosper, are worth study. Because there is one truism in the firearms business which it is useful to remember: what goes around, comes around. An idea which is proposed today may be theoretically sound but it may fail to gain acceptance for a number of reasons; it may be technologically impossible to manufacture, it may be economically unwise to manufacture, or it may not suit the prevailing fashions and beliefs in the military or shooting fraternities. And so it fades into obscurity. Then 20, 30, or even 50 years later the same idea will re-appear; the man who thought it up may not even be aware of its previous incarnation. But this time the current level of technology will have changed, economic circumstances may be different, or the shooters and soldiers may be thrilled by the idea. This time round it will succeed.

So while reading this narrative which plots the development of the handgun since 1900, bear in mind that some of the weapons which fell by the wayside might have picked themselves up and be limping along preparing for their second bite at the cherry, even though they may have gone through some changes. (The Webley-Fosbery system of cylinder rotation popped up on a shotgun a few years ago.) And when the new idea comes into view and is hailed as a 21st century innovation, you can look back and say "Ah, but. . ."

Apologies in advance if anyone's favorite pistol has been inadvertently omitted — it would have been impossible to describe every design and variation, and this book keeps to the main stream of development, with a few digressions to look at some of the more interesting proposals put up from time to time. And for those unfamiliar with the history of the modern handgun, may I suggest you treat this as a sort of appetizer, and if your appetite is whetted by some particular feature, then go on to satisfy it with the more solid fare of the many specialized books which devote themselves to one particular weapon or maker.

A Century of

Above Right: The Colt Officer's Target Revolver in .38 caliber. Introduced in 1904 this was generally similar to the contemporary Army Special revolver but to a better standard of finish and with fully adjustable fore and rear sights, deeply checkered grips and a carefully honed and adjusted trigger action.

Below Right: Top of the Smith & Wesson line in the 1900s was this "New Century" model, seen here in .455 caliber as purchased by the British Army in 1915. For immaculate finish, smooth action, and superb accuracy it has rarely been equaled.

In the eyes of many, by 1900 the revolver had gone about as far as it could go. The best products of the finest makers were masterpieces of precision, fit, and finish, built to a standard which is rarely seen in the 1990s. Anyone with a mint condition Smith & Wesson New Century, Webley-Wilkinson, or Colt Officer's Target Model would require a very substantial financial inducement to make him change it for a present-day product. So can it honestly be said that there has been any significant improvement in revolvers over the past century? Well, not, perhaps, in perceived quality — with a few exceptions the revolvers of the 1990s do not present themselves quite as well as did the revolvers of the 1900s. But this is only true when talking of the upper strata. One thing which has definitely improved over the years has been the average quality of revolvers. There is, today, no real equivalent for the 1890s product now familiarly referred to as "Suicide Specials," weapons made to sell for a dollar or two, weapons with false rifling at the muzzle to persuade buyers that they had a precision weapon, weapons made of the cheapest grade of steel, steel which could easily crack or break if you dropped it on a hard surface. Even the inexpensive pocket revolvers turned out on the Continent today are of respectable metal, reasonable manufacture, and safe design; if only because of the fear of litigation. We have not yet reached the point where makers are engraving "DO NOT POINT THIS AT YOUR OWN HEAD" on their products, but that time will doubtless come. . .

So how did the revolver progress through the 20th century? Considering that the automatic pistol was just finding its first foothold on the ladder in 1900, the revolver has managed to survive very well indeed. It was not until the final decades that the automatic pistol began to oust the revolver as a police weapon, and its conquest of the military world was not complete until the 1960s.

There are, if you care to be critical about it, some fundamental defects in the revolver; which, after all, is why the automatic pistol came into existence. The revolver is entirely manually operated, so that the rate of fire depends on the operator's dexterity. There is also a gas leak between chamber and barrel. The barrel sits comparatively high above the hand, so that there is a turning moment which tends to lift the muzzle on firing. It can be slow to re-load, due to the need to extract the empty cases and then fill the chambers individually. In large calibers the capacity of the cylinder is limited to six shots, or even five. And compared to a simple blowback automatic pistol, a revolver is a complex manufacturing proposition. These were some of the problems that designers thought that they might be able to address as the century began. Some were successful; others were not.

Handguns

One inventor who was working on a revolutionary revolver at the turn of the century was Colonel George Vincent Fosbery, VC. As a young officer, he had won his VC in the Umbeyla Expedition of 1863 on the North-West Frontier of India and after retiring in 1877 devoted his time to patenting various firearms inventions. In 1895 he began working on an

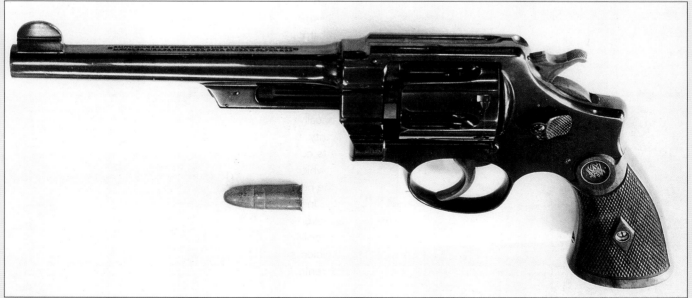

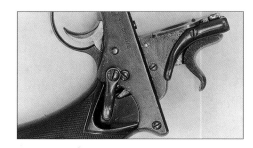

Above Right: The Wilkinson Sword Company of London supplied swords to all British officers and saw no reason why the should not also supply them with revolvers. So the Webley company made a special version of their current army revolver with a different butt, smoother trigger action, better sights, and better finish, and supplied them to Wilkinson, who then put their own name of them. British officers were allowed to purchase any revolver they wanted, provided it fired the service .455 cartridge.

Below Right: Loading a Webley-Fosbery with a Prideaux Patent Quick-Loader. This inserted all six cartridges into the chamber in one thrust, and using this enabled a Webley-Fosbery to produce a phenomenal rate of fire.

automatic revolver, one which would rotate the cylinder and re-cock the hammer after each shot without requiring the firer to do anything. All he would have to do would be to pull the trigger as fast as he could.

Fosbery's basic idea was to separate the two halves of the revolver; the butt and frame, and the barrel and cylinder. He then arranged the pieces so that the barrel and cylinder could slide back and forth across the top of the frame; and as they slid back, so they would push back the hammer and cock it. A spring would then return the unit to the firing position, leaving the weapon cocked. Fosbery's patent drawings show that he developed his working model around a Colt Frontier Model 1873 revolver. In this model, cocking the hammer would cause the cylinder to be revolved, but tests showed that this was a clumsy arrangement, and in 1896 Fosbery took out a fresh patent in which he cut an involved zig-zag groove around the outer surface of the cylinder and placed a fixed stud in the frame which was located in this groove. It is hard to resist the thought that Fosbery had seen a Mauser "Zig-Zag" revolver — this 1873 weapon had a similar pattern of grooves which engaged in a stud, but in this case the stud was pulled back and forth by the trigger, and as it moved back so it rotated the cylinder a sixth of a turn, bringing the next loaded chamber in front of the hammer as it fell. Fosbery reversed this, causing the recoil to move the cylinder across the stud, and he also halved the work-load by turning the cylinder only one-twelfth of a turn during the recoil stroke, and then another one-twelfth during the run-out movement, so that when the barrel came to rest, the fresh cylinder was aligned in front of the cocked hammer. Pull the trigger — a very light pressure — and the revolver fired, the top half slid back, the hammer cocked, the cylinder turned and turned again, and you were ready for the next shot.

Fosbery took his original idea to Webley & Scott in Birmingham, and it was there that the zig-zag cylinder was worked out and perfected. They, not unnaturally, applied Fosbery's principles to their basic Webley service Mark IV revolver, and in 1901 put the first Webley-Fosbery revolver on the market in .455 caliber. It was an immediate success, particularly with target shooters, since the recoil was rather less than normal due to the movement of the barrel unit, and after a while it was banned from military competitions since it was felt to give the firer an unfair advantage over those shooting standard revolvers. After the .455 model, a .38 model was produced. This still used the components of the service .455 revolver as its foundation, so it was able to have an eight-chambered cylinder, and it became even more popular with target shooters due to even lower recoil. Improved models followed, the improvements being minor, and after Fosbery's death in 1907 Webley continued to produce and improve the design until 1914. Production then stopped, since the

Above: A contemporary advertisement for the Webley & Scott automatic pistols and the Webley-Fosbery revolver.

company was swamped with Army contracts for standard revolvers, and it was never resumed, the Webley-Fosbery proving too expensive a product in the post-war years. The only drawback to the design was that servicemen in the trenches in 1914–18 indicated a liability to stoppages due to mud and dirt in the cylinder grooves, but those who took care of the weapon appear to have had nothing but praise for it.

A similar, but simpler and cheaper, revolver was also developed in the USA. This was by the Union Firearms Co. of Toledo, Ohio, who built a pocket pistol in .32 caliber to the designs of one C.A. Lefever. He patented a design in 1909 in which the cylinder had a much simpler zig-zag which revolved it one-fifth of a turn during the recoil stroke (it was a five-chambered cylinder) and did not move during the return. This was made possible by the smaller dimensions and thus the lesser weight and effort required. Very few of these appear to have been made before the company ceased trading some time in 1914.

There was one other fundamental defect of the majority of revolvers in 1900. If you were thumbing back the hammer to cock the weapon, and your thumb happened to slip, the hammer would go forward and fire the cartridge in the chamber. Unless, that is, you happened to have a revolver made by the Iver Johnson company. In 1897, they had patented their "Hammer the Hammer" safety system. In this, the firing pin was removed from the hammer, where it had been ever since the revolver was invented, and placed in the standing breech. The rear face of this and the front face of the hammer, were designed so that the hammer fell and actually struck the breech fame without touching the firing pin. But attached to the trigger mechanism was a "transfer bar" which, when the trigger was

properly pulled, slid up behind the firing pin so that when the hammer fell it struck the transfer bar, which thus delivered the blow to the firing pin. It was a simple and effective design which boosted Iver Johnson revolver sales.

In 1905, Colt produced their own version of this safety system, which they called the "Positive Lock." This was a small link attached to the trigger mechanism which, when the mechanism was at rest, reached up in front of the hammer and prevented it from coming forward far enough for the firing pin to hit the cartridge in the chamber. Only by pulling the trigger all the way back was this link withdrawn so as to allow the hammer a free fall. Thumb-cocking was still possible, but if the thumb slipped the link was in the way and the hammer never met the cartridge. Colt applied this to all their new revolvers, and, to make sure the customers knew about it, changed the names, so that the New Pocket model became the Pocket Positive, and the New Police model became the Police Positive.

Below: A Colt .32 caliber Police Positive revolver. This model came in a variety of calibers and barrel lengths to suit all tastes, but they all had the Positive hammer safety device which prevented the pistol firing unless the trigger was properly pulled through.

Close-ups of the opened cylinder of a Smith & Wesson "Triple Lock" revolver. The ejector sleeve locks into the front end of the shroud, the crane locks into the frame in front of the cylinder, and the ejector rod locks into the standing breech. A superlative system but very difficult to make and adjust so that all parts bore an equal share of the load.

Smith & Wesson, meanwhile, were more concerned with getting the cylinder properly locked to the frame. Those models on sale in 1900 had the cylinder retained in place simply by a stud entering the rear face of the cylinder axis rod. Pressing a catch forward withdrew this stud and allowed the cylinder to be swung sideways out of the frame for ejection of the spent cases and reloading. In 1902, they patented a new system in which the cylinder axis and hand ejector rod had a central locking pin throughout their whole length; a lug was forged under the barrel and fitted with a spring-loaded pin. A second spring-loaded pin was placed in the center of the standing breech. As the cylinder was closed into the frame, the front end of the ejector rod connected with the barrel lug, and the spring pin pressed into the hollow end of the ejector rod, pushing the central locking pin back so that it, in turn, pushed on the spring loaded pin and went into the standing breech. The cylinder and ejector unit were now solidly locked front and rear, and the system has been applied to Smith & Wesson revolvers ever since.

With that out of the way they could now turn to consider Iver Johnson's Hammer the Hammer and Colt's Positive Lock, and do something about it. Their answer was a little component called the rebound slide which, connected to the hammer, slid back and forth inside the frame and, when the trigger was forward, fouled the bottom of the hammer so as to prevent it falling far enough to fire the cartridge. Only with the trigger pulled was the rebound slide removed from the hammer path. That improvement appeared in 1906 and, again, has been an integral part of their revolvers ever since.

Finally, in 1907, Smith & Wesson took another look at locking the cylinder into the frame. For their heaviest revolvers they felt that perhaps a little extra insurance was no bad thing and they developed their famous "Triple Lock." This placed a third lug in the pistol frame, just ahead of the cylinder, which firmly held the moving arm of the crane as the pistol was closed. It was linked to the movement of the central locking pin so that a single pressure of the thumb-piece unlocked all three locks to open the pistol. Undoubtedly the safest and most elegant method of locking a side-swinging pistol, it failed to survive because it was simply too time-consuming and expensive to manufacture, and, as experience proved, not really essential.

In 1914, the world went to war, and the gunmakers had their hands full with more important matters than developing revolvers. What they already had drawings for was good enough, and all the various armies wanted was as many of them as possible. This led to an interesting piece of development in the USA. The US Army had, in 1911, settled on the Colt automatic pistol as their standard sidearm, as will be related further on; but production was in the order of 150-200 pistols a week, and once

the US government decided to expand its army, it needed pistols at a much faster rate than that. As an interim measure they asked Colt and Smith & Wesson for .45 revolvers; but (and this was the catch) they had to fire the .45 automatic pistol cartridge, because that was the standard issue sidearm cartridge.

The problem was that the auto pistol cartridge had no rim, and therefore if it was dropped into an ordinary .45 revolver chamber it simply fell straight through; somehow, it had to be stopped in the correct place for

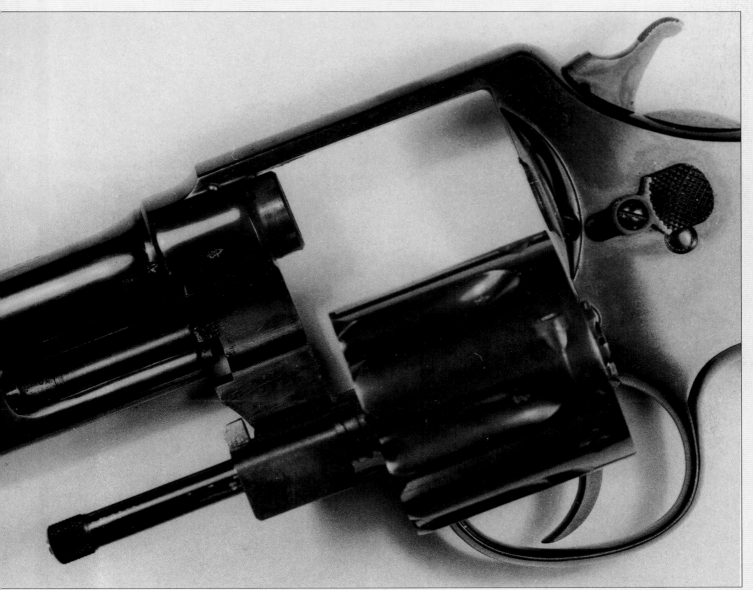

Above and Above Right: The US Army's M1917 revolvers, by Smith & Wesson (above right) and Colt (above), were their standard models but firing the .45 Auto Pistol cartridge from a special cylinder.

Below Right: The Webley & Scott Mk. I entered service with the British Army in 1887. Over the years it would be redesignated No. 1 Mk. II and see service well into the second half of the 20th century.

the firing pin to hit the cap. The two pistol makers put their heads together and came up with a simple solution — they shortened the cylinder of their standard .45 revolver, and then made semi-circular clips which held three .45 auto cartridges by their extraction groove. Two clips of three were dropped into the revolver chambers, and the thickness of the clip positioned the cartridge correctly for firing. On opening the chamber and pressing the extractor, the clips allowed the empty cases to be pushed out. You then had to pick them up and remove the clip so you could put three more cartridges in, but that was a minor problem. Colt and S&W both converted their standard revolvers in this manner and they became the "US Revolver M1917." After the war thousands were released to the civil market, and the ammunition makers promptly made a new cartridge, the .45 Auto Rim, which was the .45 auto case but with a thick rim; this loaded into the chambers of the M1917 just like any ordinary revolver, but the thick rim located the caps at the correct distance from the firing pin.

World War I saw the first large-scale use of automatic pistols in warfare, and they acquitted themselves well; so well, that in the 1920s nobody gave a great deal of thought to revolver design, being more concerned with developing automatic weapons. As with most firearms, however, a number of people realized that the best way to improve the weapon was to improve the ammunition, and in the 1930s this philosophy began to be applied to revolvers.

As is often the case, particularly in the USA, the movement began by private individuals experimenting with increased loads with a view to obtaining better performance from existing revolvers. But, as is also often the case, once the ammunition manufacturers saw what was going on, they joined in and, in the process, pulled the gunmakers in as well. The first result of this was the introduction of the Smith & Wesson .357 Magnum revolver and its associated cartridge in 1935. As far as the revolver went, there was no new technology; it was simply made stronger than the normal .38, and the cartridge was made a fraction of an inch longer than the normal .38 cartridge, so that it could not be loaded into ordinary .38 revolvers. (Bear in mind that the caliber of all so-called .38 revolvers is actually .357. The .357 Magnum got its name in order to mark it out from the common run of .38 rounds.) For the next 20 years this was the most powerful handgun cartridge in the world, and other gunmakers were soon making revolvers to suit.

This, no doubt, would have started a rush to out-do the .357, but before this came to anything World War II intervened, and, like Webleys in 1914, the gunmakers found they had more important things to do.

In Britain, the change of ammunition was in the opposite direction. For years the standard military revolver had been the .455 Webley. It was an

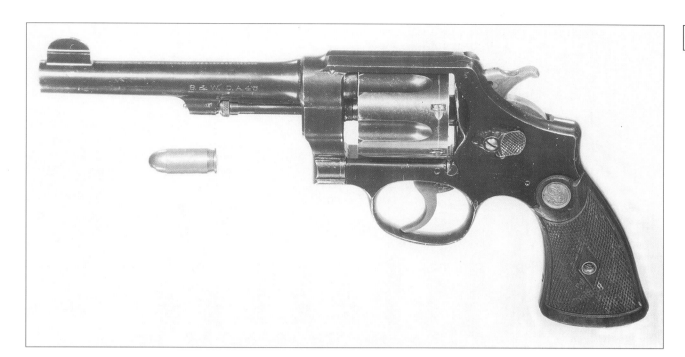

Above Right: When war gobbles up weapons, you have to use what you can get. This is the "Sealed Pattern" of a Spanish .455 revolver adopted by the British Army in 1915 as the Pistol, Old Pattern, No. 1 Mk. 1. It was made by the Garate y Anitua Company of Eibar, Spain, a top-break design copied from the old pattern of Smith & Wesson revolver popular in the early 1890s.

Below Right: Smith & Wesson .38-200 British service revolver.

excellent man-stopper but it was heavy and needed considerable practice before it could be mastered. Such practice was not possible under the stress of war, where soldiers were going from civilian to front line in three months or less. There was barely enough time to teach them the basics, let alone allow them infinite practice with a revolver. So after the war, when the matter was considered, the solution arrived at was to reduce the service caliber to .38. The experts assured the soldiers that by using a 200-grain lead bullet with a suitable charge, the .38 would have just as much stopping power as the .455, which was so obviously false that the soldiers thought it must be true — otherwise nobody would suggest such a thing. In fact, and without going too deeply into it, it can be easily shown that the .455 bullet had 253 foot-pounds of energy, while the .38 had only 155 foot-pounds. But since this was quite sufficient to knock down most opponents, and the revolver would be easier to train on and fire accurately, the deed was done and a new .38 revolver requested. Webley put forward a design which was more or less the .455 reduced in size, but this was turned down — the government small arms design office were going to do this one. Two years later they produced a revolver which was so close a copy of the Webley that Webley promptly brought a lawsuit — and won. The only significant difference lay in the trigger mechanism; but in spite of Webley's objections, the Enfield pistol went into production.

When World War II arrived, the Enfield small arms factory was busy making Bren machine guns and similar articles and had no capacity to expand production of revolvers; so the army had to go cap in hand to Webley and ask for the original Webley design to be put into mass production. Webley's, doubtless laughing to themselves, proceeded to turn out 159,000.

World War II saw no advance in revolver design or ammunition; indeed, it began the move away from revolvers in major armies, as the British began to use the Browning High-Power in small numbers and the Soviets began to abandon their 1895 Nagant revolver for the Tokarev automatic.

The years since 1945 have seen a vast surge of innovative design in automatic pistols, as we shall shortly see, but there have only been two serious attempts to produce a new form of revolver. The first was a revolver by courtesy only, since it used a revolving ammunition feed but little else that was traditional. This was the Dardick pistol, which appeared in 1954; it was in the general shape of a revolver, but instead of a cylinder there was a three-lobed "star wheel" which looked rather like a shamrock when viewed from either end. The cartridges were triangular in section — in fact they were usually standard commercial cartridges pressed into a triangular plastic sleeve, and they were loaded into the butt by means of a fairly conventional magazine. At the top, the cartridge

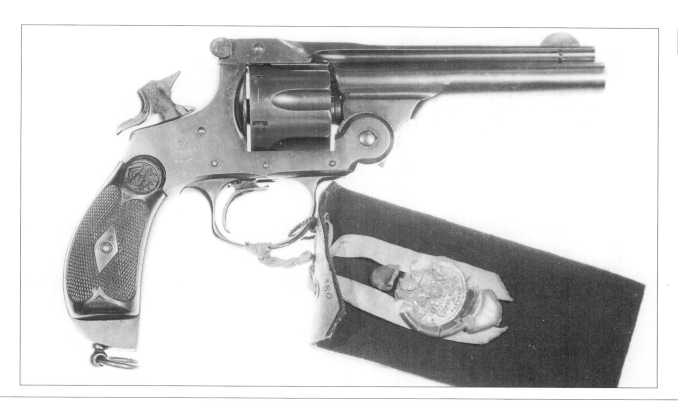

Below: The .38 Enfield revolver, adopted in preference to the .455 as it was easier to teach soldiers to shoot straight with it. Note that this is the Mk. I* model with the hammer spur removed, so that it is "double-action only." This modification was done because tank crews kept catching the hammer spur on the hatch edges as they clambered in and out of their tanks.

passed into a cut-out of the star wheel and as the trigger was pressed the wheel revolved and brought the cartridge behind the barrel as the hammer fell. During this rotation the next cartridge was taken from the magazine by the next cut-out.

The significant point about this design was that the cartridges were not, as in a revolver chamber, completely enclosed. The star wheel only supported two sides of their triangular section, the third being covered only by a thin shield which prevented them dropping out. The resistance to the cartridge explosion pressure was provided by the plastic sleeve. And as the trigger was pressed for the next shot, the sleeve moved round to the right-hand side of the gun where the thin shield was cut away, so that the empty case — or "Tround" as Dardick called it — fell clear of the gun. Produced in .38 caliber, the Dardick worked well enough but

the ammunition was not readily available and it was expensive, about a third more expensive than a comparable Colt revolver. Production ended in 1962.

The second major innovation appeared in Italy. The Mateba revolver was designed for international rapid-fire competitions; its designer, Emilio Ghisoni, saw that the principal drawback was that a conventional revolver had its barrel well above the firer's hand, thus developing a considerable turning motion which pulled the barrel up and off target on firing. So he designed a revolver with the barrel set very low over the hand and the cylinder, therefore, was low-set in front of the trigger guard. The first model to appear, in 1983, was an eight-shot in .38 Special caliber, and it was followed by a 12-shot model in either .38 Special or .357 Magnum. Next came a 20-shot .22. Then, in 1985, came a new design in which the cylinder was in the more conventional place above the trigger but the barrel was aligned with the bottom chamber, and the cylinder hinged upwards when opened, probably the only revolver which ever did so.

The idea was sound enough, and the workmanship impeccable, but although the pistols remained in limited production for some years, they appear to have ceased some time in the early 1990s. Since then there has been no notable movement in the revolver business. Today's improvements are more concerned with keeping the price down to a reasonable level by means of investment casting and computer-controlled machine tools than with attempting to re-invent the gun.

The Automatic Pistol

The automatic pistol had its foot firmly in the door by 1900. The Mauser was in production, various Bergmann models were appearing for the home defence market, and, perhaps the most significant military indication, the Swiss were about to take the decision to adopt the Luger Parabellum pistol for their army. And in 1900 the first Browning automatic pistol appeared from the Liege factory of Fabrique National, the first of a series of pistols which, by the 1930s, would make the word "Browning" synonymous with "automatic pistol" throughout Europe and much of the rest of the world.

John Browning, the American gun genius, had spent most of the 1890s designing automatic pistols and took out a number of patents in 1897. He approached Colt, who expressed an interest in his heavy-caliber locked breech ideas but not for his small-caliber blowback pistols. Coincidentally the commercial director of Fabrique Nationale (FN) of Liege, Belgium, visited the USA, met Browning and came to an agreement whereby FN would make the blowback design. Browning gave FN a hand-made model, the FN engineers turned it into a production proposition, and in 1900 it was accepted by the Belgian Army as their official sidearm in 7.65mm (.32) caliber. The 1900 model was popular, but most military customers wanted something of larger caliber, so Browning came back with a fresh design which, into the bargain, was easier to manufacture. This was the 9mm Browning Long caliber, a cartridge which was adjudged to be the most powerful that could be managed in a plain blowback

Below: A typical Bergmann design of the mid-1890s. These appeared in all calibers from 5mm to 11mm, but only the small ones had any success.

pistol, and it went on the market as the Model 1903. By this time Colt and FN had come to an agreement over Browning's designs — Colt would make them in the USA for the western hemisphere, FN in Belgium for the rest of the world, so the 1903 also appeared in the USA under the Colt name as the Colt .38 automatic.

The Model 1903 was so simple that it was seized on by Spanish gunmakers. At that time the Spanish patent laws were such that any article not actually officially sold in Spain could be copied and produced there, and since the gunmakers were quick off the mark and began making copies before FN got as far as Spain with their marketing, there was not much they could do about it. And so copies of the 1903, mainly in 7.65mm caliber, since that was more popular for personal defence, appeared under every conceivable name. Some were good, many were terrible, but they sold by the tens of thousands until the Spanish Civil War put an end to the trade in 1936.

Above: Inside a modern automatic pistol, showing magazine storage in butt. This is an ITM AT88S. Compare this with the illustration on page 24 to see how little has changed since the 1900 model.

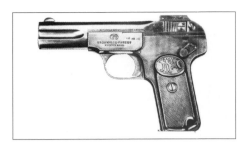

Above: John Browning's Model 1900, or "Old Model" as it came to be known, was the first commercially successful automatic pistol.

Below: A sectioned drawing of the Browning 1900 model, showing the simplicity of the design, and how it used the recoil spring as a firing pin spring.

But, attractive as the commercial market was in the 1900s, when few countries had any regulations against the ownership of personal firearms, the thing which attracted most manufacturers was the thought of a fat military contract which, as well as making them a substantial profit, would also act as a confirmation of the efficiency of their pistol and thus encourage others to buy it. The principal problem was that most military forces were wedded to heavy revolver calibers, their experience in colonial warfare having shown that only a slow-moving heavy lead bullet had the necessary force to stop an enemy in his tracks — and the automatic pistols which had appeared so far were too complex or frail to handle such potent cartridges. So, like the British in the 1930s did with their revolver, the designers convinced themselves that reducing the caliber and increasing the velocity would maintain the striking energy at a knockdown figure. This led to some spectacularly horrible designs.

Take, for example, the Mars, developed by a Mr Gabbet-Fairfax in Britain. To quote a contemporary trade magazine "His ideals wandered in the direction of high velocity and his pistols took on the appearance of

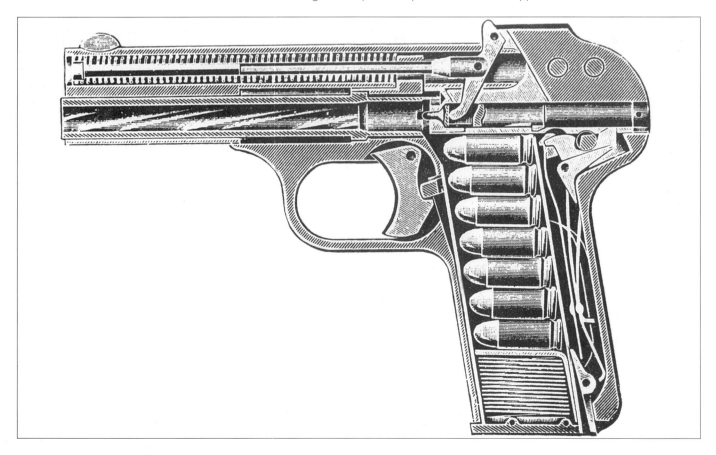

Above: The Browning Model 1903 was even more simple in construction than the Old Model and was undoubtedly the most-pirated design of pistol in history.

Left: The British "Mars" pistol firing a 9mm cartridge, the most powerful automatic pistol ever made in that caliber.

young cannon." The Mars pistol employed the principle of "long recoil" in which the barrel and breech bolt, firmly locked together, recoiled for about two inches across the pistol frame. They then came to rest, the bolt was rotated and held, and the barrel ran forward again to the firing position. As it did so, the spent case was extracted from the chamber and knocked free of the pistol by a mechanical ejector. A "cartridge lifter" now pulled a fresh cartridge from the magazine — backwards — and hoisted it up into the feedway. By this time the firer had recovered his

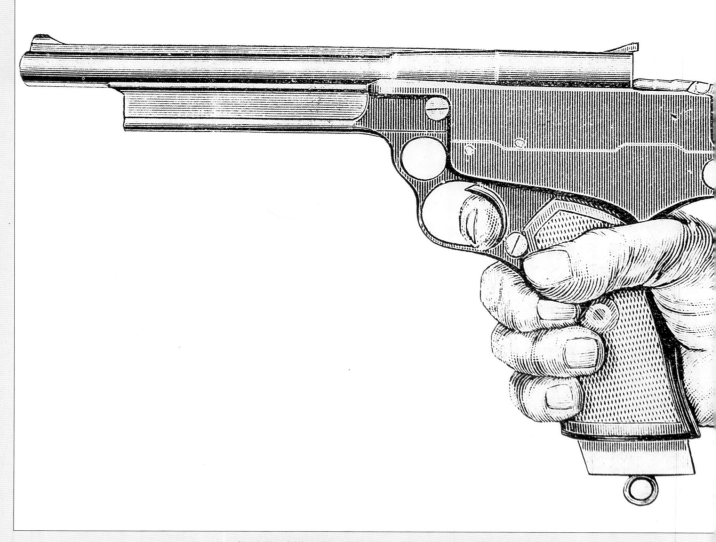

Above: A contemporary drawing showing the Mars after firing. The firer is still holding the trigger back; the barrel has recoiled, the breech has unlocked and stayed still, and the barrel has gone back to its forward position. The next cartridge has been drawn backwards out of the magazine and now rests in the feedway. When the dazed firer releases his grip, the bolt will go forward, loading the cartridge and leaving the hammer cocked ready for the next shot.

composure and released his grip on the trigger; this released the bolt, which ran forward, collected the fresh round, chambered it, and then revolved to lock the breech, leaving the pistol with its hammer cocked, ready to fire again. The Mars was made for Gabbet-Fairfax by Webley of Birmingham and appeared in 1900 in 8.5mm, 9mm, and .45 calibers, the cartridges also having been designed by Gabbet-Fairfax and considerably more powerful than anything else in those calibers. Until the Auto-Mag appeared over 50 years later, the 8.5mm Mars was the world's most powerful handgun. It was certainly too powerful for the War Office; their testers found it practically uncontrollable and refused it. The Mars company went bankrupt but it reappeared a few years later in different hands and tried again, with no more success, and finally vanished in 1907.

The Schouboe pistol, the invention of a Dane of that name, approached the solution from another direction. If the military wanted large calibers, fine; but he wanted a simple blowback pistol with no breech lock. On the face of it, the two are incompatible, since a big heavy bullet means a powerful charge and thus demands a locked breech. But Schouboe made an exceptionally light bullet from wood and aluminium.

This left the barrel at 495 meters a second, so that it was out of the muzzle before the blowback breech began to open, but like all light bullets it soon lost velocity and, as the twist of rifling was badly chosen, it was also inaccurate. No army would accept this, so the Schouboe ended up being presented to Danish Army cadet officers as graduation prizes.

One man who got it right but still lost out was Theodor Bergmann of Berlin. He had developed some practical blowback pistols in the late 1890s and then set about making a heavy military model which he (confusingly for historians) called the "Mars." It was actually designed by Louis Schmeisser (who was later to become famous for designing the first real submachine gun) and a 10mm caliber version was tried by the British in 1903. Not being the desired .455 caliber, it was refused, but the Spanish Army tried it in 9mm caliber, liked it, and gave Bergmann a contract. But just at that moment, disaster struck; Bergmann's factory was more of a development unit than a production unit, and he contracted his pistol manufacture to the firm of V.C. Schilling of Suhl, a famous gunmaking town. In 1904 Schilling's was bought out by another firm, Krieghoff, who now told Bergmann that they would cancel the contract when it fell due for renewal in 1905. So there was Bergmann with a big pistol contract and nowhere to make it. He sold the contract to Pieper, a Belgian gunsmith, and left the pistol business. Pieper called the gun the Bergmann-Bayard, "Bayard" being his trademark, and after completing the Spanish contract, proceeded to outfit the Danish Army with the same pistol.

By this time the German Navy had adopted the Parabellum pistol. This originated as the Borchardt in 1893, and had then been redesigned

Below: The Danish Schouboe was an early attempt to make high velocity into an effective man-stopper by firing a very light bullet. It failed.

Above: Mauser 7.63mm Model 1912 fitted with wooden stock.

Above Right: The German Army's Pistole '08, or Parabellum, or Luger, in 9mm caliber. First issued in 1908 many were still in first-line use in 1945, although officially replaced by the Walther P'38.

Below Right: The Long Pistole '08 or Artillery Model Luger, with long 8in barrel, wooden shoulder stock that doubles as a holster and 32-round "Snail" magazine.

by Georg Luger. The Swiss had accepted it but the German forces balked at the caliber of 7.65mm, claiming that it was insufficient for a combat pistol. Luger, certain that he had a good design, obliged by opening up the mouth of the bottle-necked 7.65mm cartridge case and putting a 9mm bullet into it. The bullet was half-conical and with a flat tip and appeared to be all that was required so far as stopping power went, and in 1904 the Navy went for it. This put the Army on its mettle and, after some more tests and discussions, in 1908 they adopted the Parabellum as the Pistole '08.

The Austro-Hungarian Army had also taken to the automatic, in a somewhat idiosyncratic way. In 1907, they had adopted the Roth-Steyr, a cumbrous pistol with a complex mechanism, the breech locked by a rotating barrel. In 8mm caliber, it was a self-cocking pistol: pulling the trigger first cocked the firing pin and then released it; it was said that this prevented a cavalry trooper accidentally firing his pistol should his horse turn restive at a crucial moment. No hair trigger, no accidental discharge. There may have been some truth in this but it made for a dismal trigger-pull.

And finally the Americans, whom you might have thought would have been in the forefront of this new technical advance, finally made their choice and after fine-tuning and altering Browning's original ideas they produced the Colt Model of 1911 automatic pistol in .45 caliber. Like other armies who had experience of fighting fanatical tribesmen of various sorts, the US Army had concluded that nothing below .45 inch was going to stop a crazed and determined enemy intent upon impaling a soldier on his spear, and after a brief flirtation with the .38 Special cartridge they had developed a potent round for their new automatic pistol.

And so, when the world went to war in 1914, the automatic pistol had a reasonable representation on the battlefield, and in spite of the

COLT
Automatic Pistol
Caliber .45

One-Half Size

The Most
Powerful Small Arm
Ever Produced

Above: An advertisement from 1906 for the new Colt automatic pistol, designed by John Browning. With some refinement and modification, it became the US Army's standard sidearm.

prevailing mud and filth of Flanders. They generally acquitted themselves well. Certainly no army which used them came out of the war itching to go back to using revolvers, and some revolver owners took a second look at the automatic pistol. Some didn't — The Birmingham Small Arms company, after assessing the wartime reports, developed what appears to have been a very good automatic in .40 caliber and offered it to the British Army. They looked at it and then returned it with the usual reply; sorry, nothing less than .455 is acceptable. And after doing that they began contemplating a .38 revolver, because experience had shown that hastily trained wartime soldiers had never enough practice with a .455 to hit what they were aiming at most of the time.

During the 1920s a number of designers began looking at automatic pistols, but the mood of the times was against them. The war to end all wars had just finished, peace and a return to normal was the watchword, and most of the world's armies were living on a shoestring. There was no development money forthcoming from the military, and most commercial manufacturers were reluctant to invest such a chancy market proposition as an automatic pistol. Except in Spain — there the manufacturers were turning out automatic pistols like there was no tomorrow.

The reason for this was that back in 1915 the French Army, desperately short of pistols, had looked to Spain for supplies. And the Spanish were able to meet that demand because of two things: firstly, the Spanish patent laws of the time allowed manufacturers to copy anything which was not patented in Spain, and secondly the gunmaking industry, concentrated around the Basque town of Eibar, was largely one of small firms relying on cheap labor and simple machinery. With the consequence that when the Browning 1903 pistol appeared in Spain, and before it was patented, the Eibar gunmakers seized on it as a simple design which they could manufacture cheaply and easily. They began making cheap copies of the Browning and when the French appeared in 1915 the Eibar industry was capable of turning its hand to the production of a standard model 7.65mm blowback pistol by the tens of thousands. The actual prime contract went to a company called Gabilondo, for their "Ruby" pistol in 7.65mm Browning caliber; but they were overwhelmed by the quantity demanded and sub-contracted much of the work. The

Above: The US Army Colt M1911A1 pistol appeared in 1923, incorporating lessons learned in World War 1, and served until the 1980s. It is still sold commercially.

Left: The first automatic pistol adopted by a major power was this Roth-Steyr, taken into service in 1907 by the Austro-Hungarian Army. A remarkable design, firing a unique 8mm cartridge, specimens were still in use in the Balkans into the 1950s.

sub-contractors found sub-sub-contractors, and by 1916 most of Eibar was turning out Ruby pistols, because the Italian Army had also arrived with a fat contract. And when the war ended there were all these small firms set up to make 7.65mm automatic pistols, with their machinery paid for and a cheap labor force standing idle. So they changed the name on their particular pistol and went into business, selling automatic pistols at prices nobody else in the world could match. Some were good, most were poor, some were distinctly horrible, but they sold. So the commercial automatic pistol market was a difficult one.

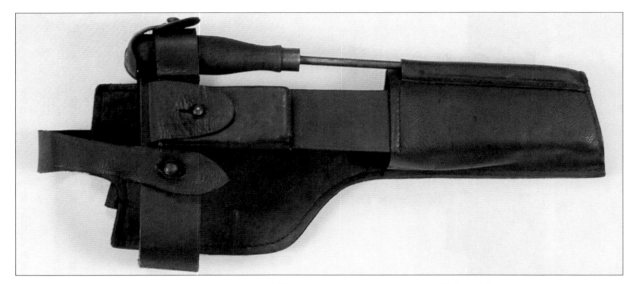

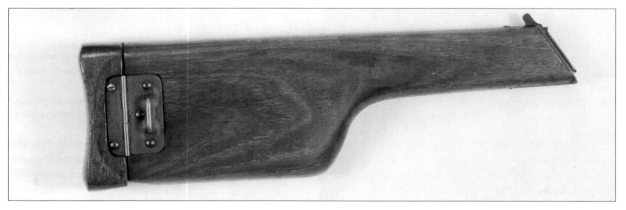

Above: Mauser 7.63mm Model 1912 complete with wooden butt/holster and clip of dummy cartridges.

But the bigger companies, in other parts of the world, those with some capital behind them, quietly went on developing, convinced that one day the sun would shine and they would be able to sell pistols. Among them was FN of Belgium, to whom John Browning had come as soon as the war was over, with some ideas for a military pistol. Having seen his design accepted by the US Army as the Colt M1911, like all designers he wasn't quite satisfied and set about improving it. Colt were quite happy with what they had, so Browning went to FN with his ideas.

The principal change was the do away with the loose link that held the barrel to the frame of the pistol and so drew the barrel back and down during recoil to unlock it from the slide. This now became a lump of metal beneath the rear end of the barrel into which a carefully calculated cam path was cut. This rested on a pin running across the frame, and as the barrel recoiled backwards so the cam, acting on the pin, caused the barrel to be drawn down to unlock it, just the same action as the link but simpler, easier to make and nothing to go wrong. He also used an internal striker, or firing pin, instead of a hammer, and had designed a new method of linking the trigger to the striker which prevented firing unless the breech was fully closed.

However, FN had a brilliant designer in-house — Dieudonne Saive was to make his name better known in later years with his automatic rifles, but he took Browning's design and suggested a few changes. Firstly he proposed a double-row magazine, giving an unheard-of 13 round capacity in the magazine. He also suggested using a hammer instead of a striker, since military customers preferred hammers — they could more easily see whether the gun was cocked. In late 1926, Browning died; Saive continued with the development of the pistol, and it was intended to announce in 1929. But the financial disasters which struck in 1929 and the economic crisis and depression which followed decided FN to postpone their new model until times were better.

Above: The 1922 Browning pocket pistol was a neat and efficient weapon.

Below: The wartime "Ruby" pistol, a copy of the Browning 1903 design, which was supplied by the tens of thousands to the French and Italian armies and which laid the foundations of countless small pistol-making companies which operated through the 1920s.

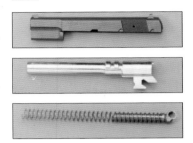

The similarity between automatics is well illustrated in these two photographs (Below and Right). Below is a field-stripped FN Mk. 3 single-action pistol.

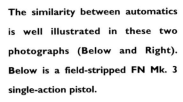

In 1934, the rumblings from across the border with Germany indicated that the time was ripe, and production of the new pistol got underway. It was announced in 1935 as the Model 1935 or High-Power and was immediately adopted by the Belgian Army, followed by various Baltic and Central European states, though they actually received few before the events of 1939 overtook them, the greater part of the production going to the Belgians.

While FN had been busy with the High-Power, the German firm of Walther had also been busy developing another milestone in the progress of the automatic pistol. They had been making pocket

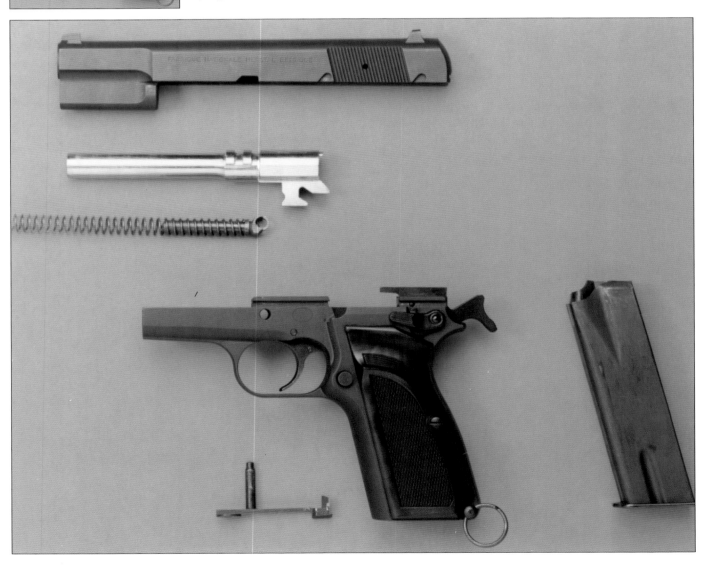

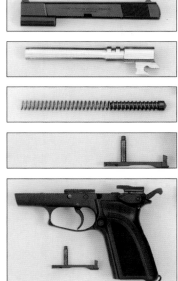

Above: A later model of the Browning High-Power, the BDA (Browning Double Action). It exhibits the same internal construction, using a shaped cam below the barrel instead of the link used on the Colt M1911.

automatic pistols since the early years of the century, but in the middle 1920s decided to produce two new models suitable for police use. By that time almost all Continental police forces had come to accept the automatic pistol as a regulation sidearm, and Walther thought that a new pistol with a novel feature would be a good seller in that market.

One of the drawbacks to the automatic pistol at that time was that you had either to carry it cocked, with a round in the chamber and the safety catch on, or you had to carry it uncocked, with the chamber empty. Which meant that when you drew it, your first movement had to be to pull back the slide (or bolt) to load the chamber and cock the pistol, before you started thinking about firing it. By which time a criminal with a cocked weapon — or a revolver — had shot you. Revolvers didn't have that problem; all modern revolvers were "double action" — you could either thumb back the hammer as you drew the revolver and simply press the trigger as you came into the aim, or you took aim and with a longer pull on the trigger, cocked and released the hammer in one movement.

So Walther took the double-action trigger of the revolver and adapted it to an automatic pistol. The Walther Model PP (for Pistole Polizei) which appeared in 1929 was an elegantly shaped weapon with a mechanism which allowed the owner to pull back the slide and load the chamber, leaving him with a cocked hammer. As he pressed the safety catch

Above Right: The Walther PPK double-action pistol, a pocket weapon for plain-clothes police.

Below Right: Compare the PPK above with the Walther PP, which was intended as a holster weapon for uniformed police.

to make the weapon safe, it first of all locked the firing pin securely, then it moved two guards around the firing pin, and finally it released the hammer, which fell against the two guards and didn't touch the pin. When the pistol was needed, as the firer drew it from its holster, so they thumbed up the safety catch, removing the two guards and unlocking the pin. They then pulled back on the trigger, just like a revolver, to cock the hammer and fire the pistol as they came into the aim. After the first shot, of course, the hammer was left cocked like any other automatic pistol; when firing was over, a pressure on the safety catch locked and guarded the pin and dropped the hammer again. So here was a weapon perfectly safe to carry, but ready to fire with the minimum of fiddling about.

It should be said that Walther did not invent the double-action mechanism for automatic pistols — it had already been produced in an Austrian pistol called the "Little Tom," the inventor's name being Tomiska. But this had attracted little attention in 1908 when he patented it, or 1920 when he manufactured it, and it remained for Walther to make a success of the idea. The PP was followed very shortly by the PPK (Pistole Polizei Kriminal — ie, pistol for the Kriminalpolizei, or plain-clothes detectives). This used a similar mechanism but was smaller, so that it could be easily concealed in plain clothes than the PP, which was intended as a holster pistol. Both soon became best-sellers, were widely adopted by police officers, and, except for a brief period after World War II, both have remained in production for the rest of the century.

Another country which decided to abandon the revolver and adopt the automatic pistol was Soviet Russia. Their principal sidearm was the 1895 Nagant revolver, an idiosyncratic weapon of doubtful efficiency, and during the 1920s a number of possible automatic pistol designs had been considered. All were of Soviet origin — it was unthinkable to adopt a capitalist design — and most were unworkable, but in 1930 the Tokarev TT-30 pistol was adopted as the official sidearm. Soviet in design it may have been, but it still relied upon the dropping barrel system patented by John Browning, though it used a solid cam under the barrel just like the Browning High-Power. The only really original idea was the assembly of the hammer and mainspring and most of the firing mechanism into a removable unit, so that repair of these parts, usually the trickiest job on any pistol, was made a great deal easier. The caliber was the standard Soviet 7.62mm; this meant that everything — pistols, rifles, machine guns — had the same caliber and therefore their barrels could be made on the same machinery, even though the actual cartridges differed. The cartridge used with the pistol was simply the 7.63mm Mauser pistol cartridge. The Soviets had acquired large numbers of Mauser military pistols and had machinery for producing the ammunition, so there wasn't a great deal of argument about adopting it as the standard cartridge. But, of course, it

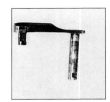

Below: The Soviet Army's Tokarev TT-33 pistol in 7.62mm caliber. Except for making the hammer and mainspring removable as a unit, the interior mechanism is the same as that of the Colt M1911.

couldn't be 7.63mm Mauser; the measurements and performance remained the same but it became the 7.62mm Tokarev or 7.62mm Pistol P when made in Russia.

The Tokarev pistol was sound and reliable, but proved a bit slow to manufacture, so in 1933 came a modification so simple that one wonders why nobody had thought of it before. Hitherto the two ribs on the barrel which locked into two recesses inside the slide had been carefully machined out of the top surface of the barrel. Now the design was changed and instead of being ribs on top of the barrel they became collars running all the way round the barrel. It sounds like a backward step, cutting away a greater quantity of metal, until you realize that the collars could be formed as the rest of the barrel exterior was formed, on a lathe, and didn't have to be transferred to a complicated milling machine in order to cut the two ribs. Speeding up production like this made a good deal of difference, though in fact it is generally agreed that only a few thousand of the original TT-30 and improved TT-33 pistols were

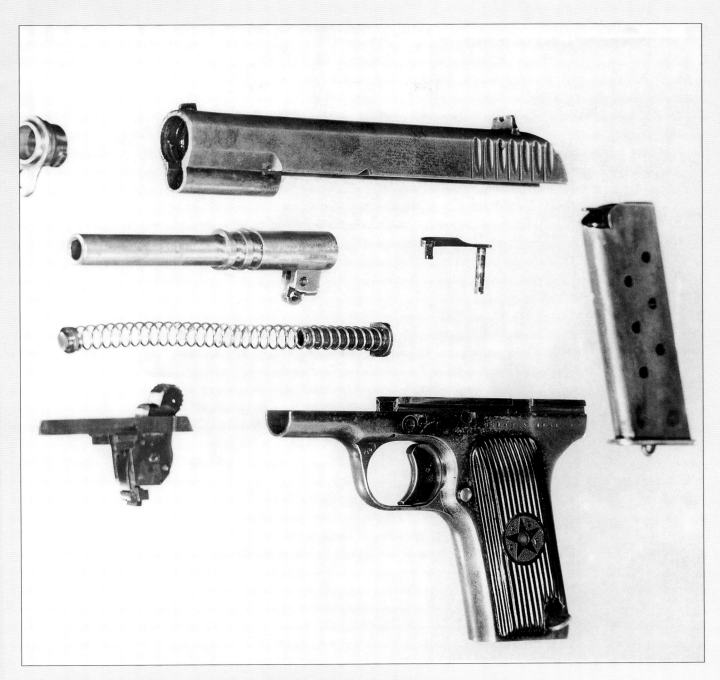

actually made before 1940. It took the impetus of the German invasion in 1941 to bring out just how much benefit the simple modification had made to production rates.

Italy had seen the virtues of the automatic pistol during World War I, when they had to buy several tens of thousands of Ruby and similar automatics from Spain. Having thus cured the immediate problem they then turned to Pietro Beretta, gunmakers since the 17th century, and asked them for a service pistol. Nothing too complex, nothing too big — they didn't have time to teach conscripts how to master heavy weapons — just something for self-defence in the trenches. Beretta produced a 7.65mm blowback of conventional form, but it had a peculiar cut-away section of the slide, for about a third of the length behind the front sight; there was then a solid portion with an ejection port and the usual rear

Above: The Tokarev TT-33 stripped for cleaning. Note the similarities with the Colt, and note also how the barrel lugs have been machined as rings around the barrel, much easier to do than milling them only on the top as in the Browning designs.

40

Below: The Beretta of 1915, showing the unusual open-topped slide, with a second opening the ejection of the empty case. The obvious manufacturing economy was to extend the cutaway portion to include the ejection port, and this has been the Beretta trademark ever since.

sight and serrated grips for the fingers when cocking the slide and hammer. Shortly after this they looked again at the design and decided that there was no point in cutting away a bit of the slide and then having to make another cut for ejection; why not simply cut away the slide all the way back to the breech? So the Model 1915/19 appeared with the top of the slide cut away over the barrel; and Beretta military pistols, by and large, have adhered to this configuration ever since, even though they now have locked breeches and are a good deal more powerful than the 1915/19 model, which was in 7.65mm caliber.

The French, who had also bought the Ruby automatic from Spain during the war, were the next to adopt one for military service. They looked at various models but, as usual, decided that a French design was mandatory. The only trouble was that there was no suitable locked breech pistol made in France, so they studied various designs on offer and took one designed by Charles Petter, a somewhat mysterious Swiss who was working for the Societe Alsacienne de Constructions Mecanique (SACM). It was little more than a variation on the Browning High-Power, though he had designed an ingenious module which allowed the entire firing mechanism to be removed for repair or cleaning as a unit — very

similar to the idea of Tokarev. On the whole it was a sound design, but it was handicapped by being built around a worthless cartridge, the 7.65mm Longue, never used by any other nation. Some writers claim that it was derived from the American Pedersen cartridge developed in World War I in an attempt to make the Springfield rifle into a species of submachine gun, but apart from some similarity in dimensions there seems no good evidence for this. It seems more likely that it was a French arsenal draughtsman's attempt to provide a 7.65mm cartridge as powerful as possible and different to that of anyone else.

The French placed a contract with SACM for the new pistol, which they called the Modele 35. The result was a well-made pistol but production was slow. So to speed things up the state arsenal at St Etienne took the basic SACM design and modified it, principally by reversing the barrel locking system by putting the lug on the slide and the recess on the barrel, instead of the universally-used lug on barrel and recess in slide. In the interests of cheaper and faster machining they made the butt straight, removed any elegant contours on the slide and allowed the barrel to protrude. Even so, the rate of manufacture was such that relatively few were in the hands of troops before war broke out in 1939.

The next to appear in 1935, a vintage year for pistols, was the Polish VIS or Radom. The Poles had inherited a miscellaneous collection of pistols from various donors after 1918, and a competitive trial was held

Above: The French M1935S pistol designed by Charles Petter. It used a 7.65mm cartridge unique to the French service. Had it been chambered for a more common cartridge it might had have more success.

Above: The Polish Radom 9mm pistol, one of the best of its class. This was made in 1938 and bears the Polish eagle on the slide. The wooden grips would appear to be a later substitution.

Far Right Above: The Radom dismantled, showing that the mechanism is just the same as that of the Browning High-Power. This version has the proper plastic grips but does not bear the Polish eagle; instead it has German Army inspection marks, and was produced in the Polish arsenal under German occupation.

in the early 1930s to settle on a standard model. The winning entry, designed by two Poles named Wilniewczyc and Skrzypinski, was another variation on the Browning basic design which, like the High-Power, used a cam beneath the barrel to unlock the breech. An unusual detail was a hammer release catch on the slide which allowed the hammer to be lowered safely onto a loaded chamber, thus permitting the weapon to be carried fully loaded but uncocked. All that was necessary was to thumb back the hammer and press the trigger. Somewhat heavier than the general run of 9mm Pistols, the Radom was one of the best combat pistols ever made. It was put into production in 1935 for the Polish Army, and when the Germans occupied the country in 1939 they kept it in production for use by their own troops, though as the war lengthened the quality suffered. Recent reports (1995) suggest that the design may be revived and put into production once again.

The last of the 1935 crop was the Finnish Lahti, resembling the Luger in outline but very different internally. Firing the 9mm Parabellum cartridge, it used a vertically sliding breech lock, and, unusually for a pistol, it also incorporated an accelerator lever which speeded up the movement of the bolt once it had been unlocked. Of superlative quality, the design is also notable for being almost impervious to dust and harsh environments, though it has been criticized on the grounds that it is almost impossible to dismantle without armorer's training and a full toolkit.

The only other design of any consequence which appeared prior to World War II was an aberrant device from Czechoslovakia, the CZ38. The CZ (Ceska Zbrojovka) company had produced a series of small pistols chambered for the 9mm Short cartridge since the early 1920s, but in 1938, in response to a request from the Czech Army, they offered a fresh and totally different design. It was a good deal bigger, as big as most pistols firing the 9mm Parabellum round, yet still chambered for the Short cartridge, and it was a blowback design. But the novelty lay in the firing mechanism; it could only fire in the double-action mode. The hammer lay forward at all times, but was kept away from the firing pin by a blocking bar and was cocked and released by a long pull of the trigger which also withdrew the blocking bar from the hammer's path. It allowed the pistol

to be carried loaded and in safety, and brought into action simply by pulling the trigger, but it was done at the expense of an abysmal trigger-pull which invariably pulled the muzzle off the target whenever the pistol was fired. As we shall see, it was a good idea, several years ahead of its time, but badly executed.

World War II saw little advance in pistol design; all the combatants had serviceable pistols at the outset and also had more important things for their design staffs to do. The only new design of any significance was in connection with the German "Volkspistole" project, itself a part of a larger program intended to furnish cheap and easily-made weapons for

Above: It looks like a Luger and it fires the same cartridge, but that's as far as the resemblance goes. The Finnish Lahti pistol, which works on an entirely different system to the Luger and was built to an exceptionally high standard to survive service in Arctic climates.

These neat little pistols are the CZ24 (Below, lower) and the CZ27 (Below, upper and Above), both in 9mm Short caliber and both used by the Czech Army and police forces in the 1930s. The difference was that the CZ24 had a locked breech and the CZ 27 didn't.

arming the "Volkssturm," a last-ditch home defence force largely of schoolboys and old men. Nothing much came of the Volkssturm or the armaments project other than the Volkspistole and a similar long arm, the Volksgewehr. The design was an attempt to solve the problem of firing a powerful cartridge in a simple weapon, in this case the 9mm Parabellum cartridge in a blowback gun. This had been done before but it demands careful manufacture from first-class material, and neither of those commodities was on offer in Germany in late 1944. The solution was to make a fixed-barrel pistol with two gas vents at the start of the rifling. The sheet-metal slide was designed to fit closely around the barrel, so that when the cartridge exploded there was a rush of gas into the space between slide and barrel. This built up pressure which tended to resist the rearward movement of the slide until the bullet was clear of the barrel and the gas could then leak back through the vents, into the barrel and out to the open air. The project got as far as prototypes, but the end of the war ended the development and it was to be several years before the idea was picked up and made to work again.

In the immediate post-war years most countries were concerned with picking up the threads of peaceful life and were little inclined to worry about pistol design, but in neutral Switzerland the war had given them cause to look to their various types of armament. Many were of foreign origin — their service pistol was the German Parabellum, albeit made in Switzerland and the Swiss Army had asked for something easier, more modern, and less expensive. The response came from the Schweizer Industriegesellschaft — better known as SIG — which had, in 1937, purchased the patents of Charles Petter, the man who had designed the French MAS 1935 pistol. With this as a starting point they set about making improvements, most of which were minor but one was fundamental. In the standard type of automatic pistol using a slide moving on top of a frame, it was normal for the slide to engage in rails or grooves formed in the outside of the frame; this was easier to make, among other things. SIG reversed this and made their slide move on rails machined inside the frame. The frame was longer than usual and the result was better support for the moving slide, giving a great deal less wear and improving the accuracy. The SIG SP47/8 (so-called from its date of introduction and magazine capacity of 9mm Parabellum cartridges) was

Above: The CZ27 was replaced by the CZ38, shown here, which fired the same cartridge. The principal drawback was that the hammer could not be cocked, and the pistol could only be fired by a long and creepy trigger-pull to raise and release the hammer.

Below: On the credit side, the CZ38 was very easy to strip and clean.

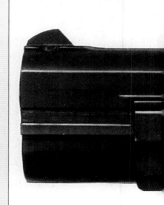

Above: The postwar Swiss pistol to replace the Luger was this SIG 8/48 model, with went into Swiss service as the Pistol 49.

adopted by the Swiss Army, then the Danish and then the West German Border Police, after which it was put on the commercial market as the SIG SP210, where it soon gained a reputation for accuracy and reliability which it has never lost. The only drawback was that it was expensive; target shooters were prepared to pay for this, but not armies, and the SP210 never achieved any further military acceptance.

After this there was a long period in which not very much happened. New pistols appeared, but only a handful showed any technical novelty. Beretta realized that the 9mm Short cartridge, which had been their standard, was now replaced by the 9mm Parabellum and therefore a locked breech pistol was needed. They responded with their 1951 model which adopted the locking block that originally appeared on the Walther P-38 pistol. The Czechs, who had by now realized the shortcomings of both the 9mm Short cartridge and the CZ38 pistol, appeared with the CZ52, which went from the extremes of simplicity to the other end of the scale and used a breech locking system which appears to have been based on that of a machine gun, two locking rollers which are moved in and out of engagement by cam tracks in the pistol frame. The lock was demanded by their adoption of the Soviet 7.62mm pistol round, which was simply a militarized version of the old 7.63mm Mauser cartridge.

Adoption of a Soviet cartridge was, of course, part of the price to be paid for falling within the Warsaw Pact bloc of countries; yet the Soviets, when they required a replacement for their Tokarev pistol, devized an

entirely new cartridge. As with most Soviet designs it was sufficiently different to make it unusable in any other weapons and prevent any other ammunition being used in Soviet weapons. The 9mm Makarov was slightly larger than the 9mm Short, and obviously designed to be as powerful as possible within the restrictions of a blowback pistol. The matching pistol, the Makarov, was very little more than a copy of the German

Below: The Pistol 49 was gradually improved and this is the final version, the SIG P-210, which replaced the Pistol 49 and was also adopted by the Danish Army. It is still made for commercial sale and is probably the finest automatic pistol in current manufacture anywhere. Notice how the slide rides inside the frame.

Above: The Russian Stechkin machine pistol with shoulder stock fitted. Like most of this class, it was uncontrollable in automatic fire unless the stock was fitted, and only just controllable then. The Russians took it out of service within ten years of adopting it.

Walther PP, and a second pistol, the Stechkin, was virtually an enlarged copy of the PP with the addition of that dubious bonus — full-automatic fire — so as to make it, in effect, a small submachine gun.

The idea of a full-automatic pistol surfaces from time to time, and the Stechkin was the first revival for many years. But although the designer doubtless thought he had hit on something new and attractive, in fact the Stechkin was simply the heir to all the objections previously observed in this class of weapon. The light weight of the recoiling parts means a very high rate of fire and, as a result, the weapon is virtually uncontrollable; it may be useful to spray a burst of unaimed shots in the general direction of the enemy, but as a weapon for precise shooting it is a failure. The Stechkin was issued with a removable shoulder stock, and the official handbook recommended its use whenever possible, but in spite of this the experiment was a failure and it was withdrawn from service within a few years of its introduction.

After that things were relatively quiet until the 1970s, when terrorism began raising its head more frequently and police forces, who hitherto regarded the pistol as a dress ornament or a method of subduing the occasional gangster, found that they needed more firepower. Moreover, they demanded foolproof firepower — they wanted a pistol that was safe to carry loaded but did not require both hands to prepare it for use and did not require complicated sequences of push, pull, and twist to operate any safety devices; a pistol which would infallibly knock down a miscreant but, miraculously, leave the innocent unharmed. They also wanted ammunition which would never ricochet into an innocent bystander but which would penetrate motor car doors to incapacitate the escaping terrorist or which could be discharged inside an aircraft and kill a hi-jacker but not penetrate the pressure cabin — the list was endless and impossible, but it put a lot of designers on their mettle and produced some striking designs.

The Heckler & Koch company were formed in Germany in the 1950s and were making the German Army service rifle, the G3. This was a descendant of an experimental Mauser design and used a roller-delayed blowback action. The firm had begun its career by making a pocket pistol, the HK4, which was more or less an improved version of a pre-war Mauser design. Faced with the challenge of a service pistol they adapted their rifle's delayed blowback action to a pistol and produced the

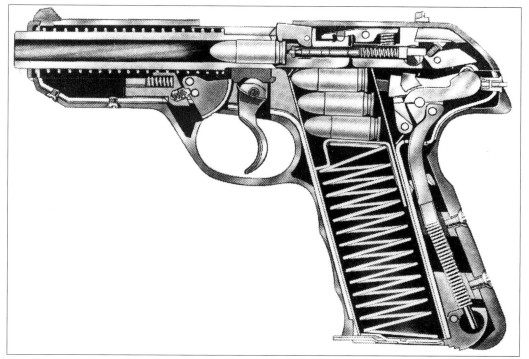

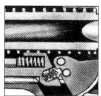

P9, a conventional single-action model in 9mm Parabellum caliber, and then followed it with the P9S which was a double-action design. However, good as these were, they came nowhere near answering the demands of the German police for their anti-terrorist pistol, and Heckler & Koch went back to the drawing board to produce the VP-70.

The VP-70 was the first pistol to employ modern synthetic ("plastic") materials to any significant extent. The frame was of synthetic material with a moulded-in barrel support and slide rails; it was fixed-barrel blow-back pistol for the 9mm Parabellum caliber and the trigger action was self-cocking (or, to use the phrase which later became fashionable, "dou-ble-action only"). The magazine held an astonishing 18 rounds, and pulling the trigger would first cock the firing pin and then, after a distinct second pressure was felt, release it to fire the pistol. So the firer could feel the point at which the firing pin was cocked and could then maintain the

Above: Heckler & Koch P9. A 9mm caliber pistol operating by delayed blowback, the delay being applied by two rollers in a similar manner to their rifle and submachine gun operation. The bolt face is separate from the slide and must force the locking rollers out of engagement with the frame before the slide can recoil.

Left: Heckler & Koch began their manufacturing career with the HK4 pistol, more or less a postwar version of the old Mauser HSc, a blow-back pistol in 7.65mm caliber.

Above: The Heckler & Koch VP-70 was, like the Stechkin, a machine pistol, but with some refinements. When set for automatic, fire would only fire a three-round burst for one pressure of the trigger and it would only do that if the butt was fixed in place, as shown here.

Right: The Heckler & Koch P7 included an ingenious innovation in the butt. The gun remained cocked for only so long as pressure was maintained on the grip.

pressure while they perfected their aim — having probably pulled off the aim during the cocking movement — and then released with a slight further squeeze of the trigger.

As if that were not enough, there was a plastic holster-stock provided; and when this was clipped to the rear of the pistol a tongue passed into the pistol's mechanism and converted the firing mode from single shot to full-automatic, so that the policeman now had a species of submachine gun. However, the full-automatic was restricted to three shots only for one pull of the trigger; after three shots the firer had to release the trigger and pull it again, having re-aimed in the interval. This made sense, because everyone who had ever tried one of this type of weapon knew that the first two or three rounds were the only ones which went anywhere near the target — the rest of the burst went into the air above the target as the pistol climbed rapidly out of control and came down about two miles away to kill some innocent pedestrian. So if it only fired three shots at a time, there was a good chance that most of the shots would arrive somewhere in the region of the target.

A good idea, but it failed to catch on. Many found the trigger pull too much for them, others complained of a lack of accuracy, and the blowback action was somewhat violent. So, back to the drawing board again and the P7 was born. This introduced a variation of the gas delay system used by the Volkspistole, though in a different manner. A vent in front of the chamber allowed gas to pass into a cylinder beneath the barrel. Into the front end of the cylinder ran a piston rod connected to the slide. Around the fixed barrel was the usual sort of return spring. On firing, the gas pressure inside the cylinder resisted the rearward movement of the piston and thus delayed the movement of the slide and the opening of the breech. It did this very successfully, moderating the violence of the blowback action, for it was chambered for the 9mm Parabellum cartridge.

In addition, there was an ingenious new cocking system. The front edge of the butt was a movable grip which, when squeezed in by the action of holding the pistol, cocked the firing pin. So long as the grip was squeezed, the weapon remained cocked, but should the holder drop it for any reason it immediately de-cocked and was in a safe condition before it landed on the ground, so that there can be no chance of an accidental discharge. Once cocked by squeezing, trigger pressure fired the

Top: The Glock 17 pistol has the frame of polymer plastic with metal cast into it, giving a light but strong structure. Notice the auxiliary switch on the trigger which acts as the safety device. Unless this is pressed into the trigger, the weapon cannot be fired.

Above: Sectioned view of the H&K P7, showing the gas cylinder beneath the barrel which resists the opening movement of the slide, and also the front grip unit which controls the operation of cocking and firing.

pistol, and provided the firer maintained their grip on the pistol, subsequent rounds were fired in the usual manner. There was no safety catch, none being necessary with this form of grip safety device.

This met all the practical requirements of the German federal police and has since been adopted by many other continental forces. The company later developed a modified version to fire the .45 Colt Automatic cartridge. This used oil in the cylinder beneath the barrel instead of gas, to form a recoil brake. It worked well, and was pleasant to fire, but failed to raise much enthusiasm in the market place and was soon abandoned.

The Volkspistole gas system was also adopted by the Austrian company Steyr-Mannlicher. They used the identical method, tapping gas out of the barrel into the interior of the slide, which fitted closely around the fixed barrel. With an 18-shot magazine, this "GB" pistol was a very accurate and comfortable weapon, the gas system soaking up a good deal of the recoil, but it was expensive and failed to attract many buyers.

When the Austrian Army decided it needed a new pistol in the 1980s, it was automatically assumed that Steyr would be given the contract and supply the GB pistol. But to everyone's surprise the contract went to an unknown company called Glock, who, hitherto, had been making knives and entrenching tools for the Austrian Army. The Glock pistol continued the trend begun by the Heckler & Koch VP70, using a good deal of synthetic material in its construction — frame and slide were synthetic, with steel inserts for friction bearing surfaces and metal for the barrel and other components. This led to a good deal of sensational scare-mongering in the popular press, to the effect that such a weapon was a gift to the terrorist, since, being plastic, it could be smuggled past airport X-Ray machines. The company soon showed that there was no substance in this nonsense, since something like 60 percent of the weapon's content was steel and it could be detected by any X-Ray machine with no difficulty.

The effects of the German police specification were also evident in the Glock, insofar as it had no conventional safety device but relied upon

Above: The Browning 9mm Mark 3 is the 1935 design brought up to date. Note that, like most modern pistols, the safety catch is duplicated on both sides so that left-handers can fire it as easily as right-handers. The magazine catch can also be changed from one side to the other.

Right: The SIG P228, one of a family of automatic pistols which look very similar. Notice the thumb-lever for de-cocking the hammer or re-cocking it, and the ejection port on top of the slide into which the barrel locks. This is a far easier manufacturing proposition that the Browning system of two lugs machined on top of the barrel and two corresponding recesses machined into the underside of the slide top.

Below: Firing the SIG P228.

a self-cocking mechanism and a small safety plate let into the surface of the trigger. Unless this plate was correctly pressed in by the action of pulling the trigger, the firing mechanism remained disconnected and the pistol would not function; pulling the trigger first cocked the firing pin and then released it, and dropping the weapon would de-cock it and also, removing pressure from the safety plate, render it incapable of firing. The Glock, which began as an unknown quantity, soon gained ground among police forces all over the world.

The SIG company in Switzerland also looked at the German specification and set about answering it in a different way. But they were confronted with a slight difficulty in the matter of the Swiss government's attitude to exporting arms; as one Swiss once said. "We are only allowed to sell arms to people who don't want them." So SIG went into partnership with the old-established German firm of J.P. Sauer & Son; SIG designed the weapons and made them for sale inside Switzerland, Sauer made them in Germany for sale outside Switzerland, and so the family of SIG-Sauer pistols came into existence.

The first was the P220 which, while conventional enough in general appearance, held a number of interesting variations. There was no safety catch; instead there was a de-cocking lever. With the pistol loaded and cocked, pressure on this lever would lock the firing pin in place and then allow the hammer to fall until stopped by a safety sear well clear of the firing pin. In addition, the firing pin was locked at all times except during the last movement of the trigger prior to releasing the hammer. The trigger allowed single or double action firing, so once the hammer had been lowered, all that was needed to fire the pistol was to pull the trigger through to cock and release the hammer. The barrel was locked to the slide not by the usual Browning lugs but by shaping the area around the chamber into a rectangle and making the ejection port in the slide cross the top of the slide to act as a locking recess for the chamber block. This gave a more robust locking area, and one which was much easier to adjust into a perfect bearing surface than the conventional interior lugs and recesses — it is noteworthy how many designers in the 1990s have copied this simple idea. Altogether, the SIG-Sauer P220 was as easy to use as a revolver, with nothing to do except de-cock it on first loading. No safety devices to worry about, and the weapon is perfectly safe unless the trigger is pressed. SIG followed it up by a range of models — the P225, 226, 228, and 229 — which are all similar in construction, differing only in size, magazine capacity, and caliber. The standard caliber is 9mm Parabellum, but 9 x 21mm and .40 Smith & Wesson are also available. These very popular SIG designs have been adopted in several armies and also by a number of American federal agencies including the Secret Service.

Above: This American Springfield P9 pistol is another CZ75 copy, with one or two minor cosmetic changes.

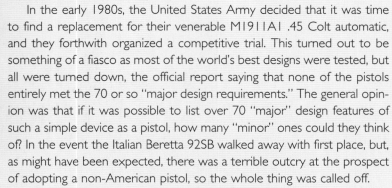

Another 1970s appearance was the CZ75 from Czechoslovakia. This was deliberately designed for the export market, since 9mm Parabellum pistols had no military future in the Warsaw Pact area. It was based on the well-proven Colt-Browning system, using lugs on the barrel to lock into the slide and a shaped cam beneath the barrel to unlock on recoil. It held 15 rounds in the magazine, balance and shape were excellent, as was the quality, and it soon found popularity in Europe and the USA. It has since been copied in Italy and the USA, and several other designs owe their inspiration to this conventional but well-made Czech design. Though even the Czechs are not proof against optimism — in the early 1990s they produced a full-automatic version for police use, though this seems not to have attracted many buyers.

In the early 1980s, the United States Army decided that it was time to find a replacement for their venerable M1911A1 .45 Colt automatic, and they forthwith organized a competitive trial. This turned out to be something of a fiasco as most of the world's best designs were tested, but all were turned down, the official report saying that none of the pistols entirely met the 70 or so "major design requirements." The general opinion was that if it was possible to list over 70 "major" design features of such a simple device as a pistol, how many "minor" ones could they think of? In the event the Italian Beretta 92SB walked away with first place, but, as might have been expected, there was a terrible outcry at the prospect of adopting a non-American pistol, so the whole thing was called off.

It did, though, focus attention on the Beretta design. This was simply an up to date version of their 1951 model, using the Walther pattern locking block, and with a double-action trigger mechanism. The design was then extended into several variations, such as the 92S with a de-cocking lever on the slide, the SB with the safety lever on both sides

Right: Beretta 9mm M92. The M92S would win the competition to replace the venerable Colt M1911A1.

Below: The British Spitfire Mark 2 was based upon the CZ75 but with added refinements to make it an excellent target pistol.

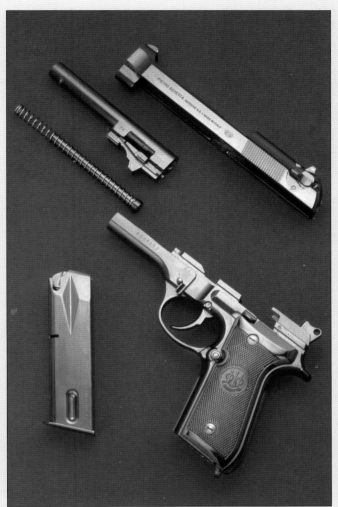

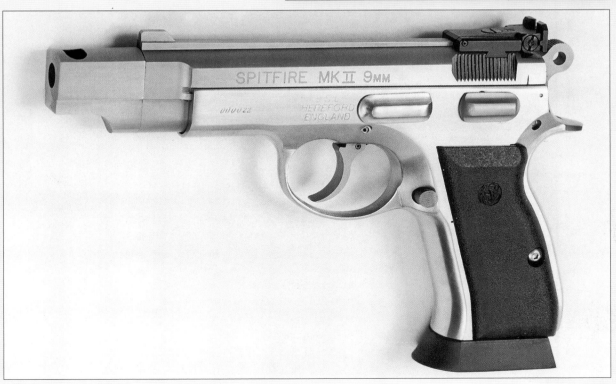

Left: The Italian Tanfoglio TA-90.

Above: The Beretta 92F, which eventually became the US Pistol M9.

Right: Two relatives of the Beretta 92F. Top, the Model 92SB Compact, and below the 92SB Compact Type M. The SB Compact has a 13-shot magazine and the Type M an 8-shot. Beretta make exactly what the customer requires.

of the slide, a magazine release which could be moved from left to right if required, and an automatic firing pin safety. In the middle 1980s the Americans once again threw open the pistol competition and it was a virtual dead-heat between a SIG design and the Beretta 92FS, which was the SB but with the trigger-guard formed for a two-handed grip, a chromed barrel, an extension to the magazine platform to give a better grip, and an anti-corrosion finish. Beretta eventually won the US contract on price, and manufacture commenced in Italy and then was transferred to a factory in the USA, the pistol being adopted as the M9. Gaining the US contract, of course, was a considerable boost to Beretta's reputation, and the 92, in various models, has been widely adopted around the world, including the French armed forces and gendarmeries.

If the US Army trial did nothing else, it certainly concentrated the minds of various American manufacturers, who had, by default, allowed

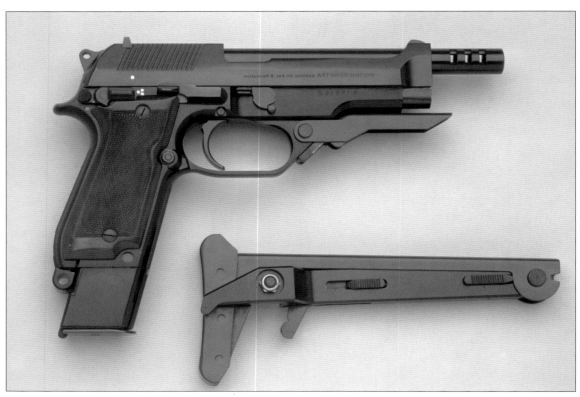

Top: Beretta also make smaller pistols; here a team of Italian policewomen practice with the 6.35mm Beretta Model 20.

Above: Beretta 93R pistol

European designers to set the pace for the preceding 20 years. Smith & Wesson had produced a 9mm double-action automatic pistol in the 1960s, but 9mm was not considered to be a worthwhile cartridge in the USA in those days and they never became very popular. But the military adoption of the Beretta and the publicity surrounding the Glock suddenly made people realize that perhaps there was something in this strange European cartridge after all, and demand for 9mm automatic pistols rapidly outstripped supply.

Sturm, Ruger & Co., hitherto renowned for an excellent .22 automatic pistol and a range of first-class revolvers, surprised many people in 1987 by producing a 9mm Automatic pistol which was as up-to-date as any gun emanating from Europe. The Ruger P85 used the familiar Browning cam to unlock the barrel, and adopted the SIG system of locking the chamber area into the ejection slot to lock slide and barrel together. The frame was of alloy, the barrel and most small parts of stainless steel, the barrel of chrome-molybdenum steel, and the safety catch could be operated from either side of the pistol. It was Ruger's bad luck that the pistol was not ready for testing when the US Army held its competitive trials, since it would undoubtedly have shown up well in the trial and had there been any shortcomings they would probably have been given time to correct

Above: Tanfolglio S Model.

Left: Field-stripped FN BDA9 double-action pistol.

Above: The Ruger P94DC, one of the many variations of their original P85 9mm pistol.

Below: The Grendel P-12.

them before a re-trial. Since the introduction, several variant models have been produced: with de-cocking levers instead of safety catches, with no single-action operation, compact models, models in .40 S&W caliber, and, in 1995, a version with a built-in laser spot projector underneath the frame. With this version all that is necessary is to switch on the laser, move the pistol until the spot of light lies on the target, and then pull the trigger. Forget the sights.

Smith & Wesson also made a major assault on the automatic pistol market in the late 1980s with their "Third Generation" series. They produced a bewildering range of models in 9mm Parabellum, .40 S&W, 10mm Auto, and .45 calibers, in standard and compact sixes; in carbon steel, stainless steel, and light alloy combinations, blued, polished, satin-finished, with adjustable sights or fixed sights — with this range the company were determined to offer something for everybody. But basically the guns were dropping-barrel locked breeches with automatic firing pin safety, ambidextrous manual safety catches, magazine safety (preventing the pistol being fired if the magazine is removed and a round inadvertently left in the chamber), and an improved bushing between the muzzle and the slide to improve accuracy.

Above: In 1990, Smith & Wesson tried again, with their "Third Generation" automatic pistols, and attained a far greater success. This is the Model 4506 in .45 caliber.

Left: The Colt 2000 appeared in 1991 and was an entirely new departure, a double-action pistol with a trigger "like a revolver," which was pulled through to fire each shot. Breech locking was by a rotating barrel. Unfortunately quality control problems dogged the initial production and it failed to sell as well as Colt had hoped. It was withdrawn from production within five years.

Right and Far Right: The FN "FiveSeveN" pistol uses an advanced form of delayed blowback operation and is largely made of synthetic materials. The 20-round magazine in the butt is comfortable to hold and the penetrative power is awesome. The inset view gives an indication of its size.

Below: The Uzi pistol is little more than a reduced-size version of the Uzi SMG but with the mechanism altered so that it can only fire in the semi-automatic mode. The design is such that it cannot be readily changed back into a submachine gun. It makes a surprisingly handy combat pistol.

Colt also looked to the 9mm automatic market and produced their All-American 2000 model, which was a considerable departure from their traditional design. It used a rotating barrel and a self-cocking firing mechanism, the object being to have an automatic pistol that could be handled and used in exactly the same manner as a double-action revolver. Unfortunately, the company appears to have had quality control problems and the pistol failed to gain acceptance in the market-place. It was withdrawn in 1994.

There is one other trend which deserves mention, and this is the development of pistols which are simply semi-automatic versions of compact submachine guns. These began to appear in the USA in the 1970s, largely as "fun guns" for people who wanted a submachine gun but were prohibited by statute from owning automatic weapons and were therefore happy to acquire a semi-automatic "look-alike." But in the late 1980s came the concept of the "Personal Defense Weapon," an extremely compact submachine gun suitable for use by non-frontline military personnel. This, in turn, has caused serious manufacturers to look at semi-automatic versions as potential pistols. The Uzi submachine gun was probably the first in this field, offering the Uzi pistol in the early 1980s. This was simply a scaled-down version of the submachine gun, capable of

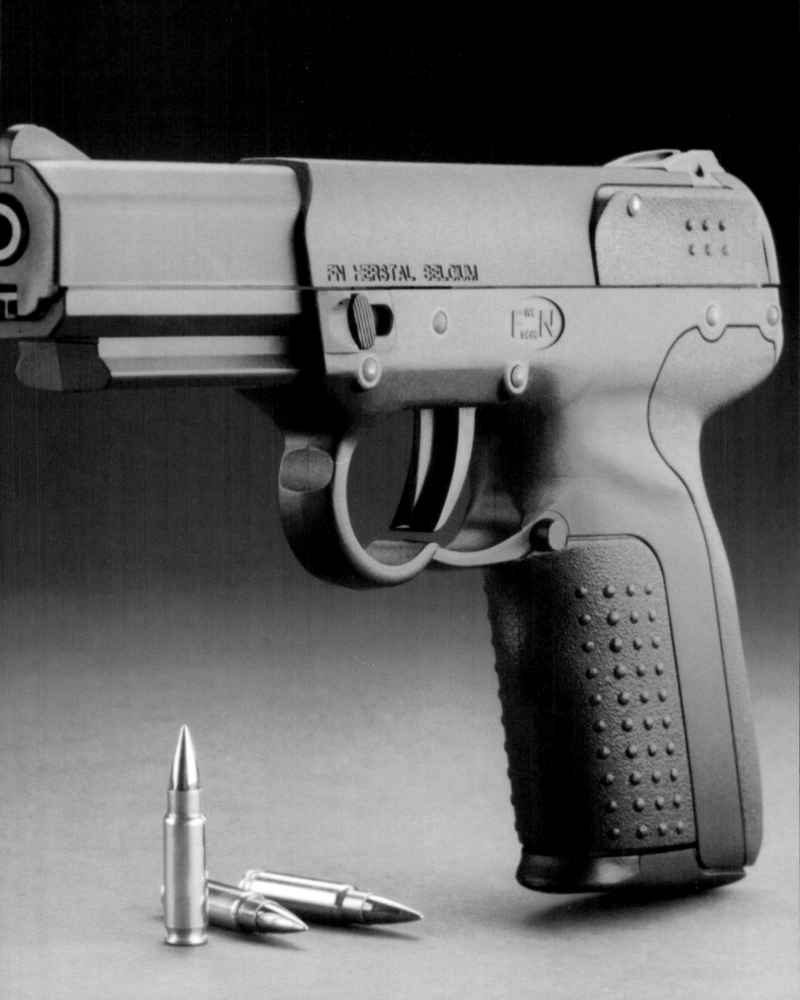

Above: FN 9mm GP Mk III single-action pistol.

semi-automatic fire only and, being of a different size, impossible to re-convert back into the automatic weapon. FN of Belgium began the Personal Defense Weapon trend with their P-90, a futuristic submachine gun firing a new 5.7mm cartridge, and followed this up with the "FiveSeveN" pistol firing the same round, though this looks more like a Browning pistol than like the original P-90 weapon. Steyr-Mannlicher of Austria produced a 9mm Tactical Machine Pistol in the early 1990s and have followed it with a Special Purpose Pistol, which is virtually the same weapon but without a front grip and firing only in the semi-automatic mode. It will be interesting to see how this movement develops.

It can be said that, at the turn of the 21st century, the automatic pistol is in much the same position as the revolver was at the commencement of the 20th century — it has reached a state of perfection that will be hard to improve upon and which will demand some inventive and innovative engineering and a great deal of capital expenditure to advance in any worthwhile degree.

Left: The US Special Operations Command (SOCOM) required a specialized pistol for raiders and other operators, which had to be of .45 caliber and have as accessories a silencer and a laser aiming spotlight. This is the Colt design, complete with its fittings.

Left: The Steyr-Mannlicher 9mm Special Purpose Pistol is another derivative from a submachine gun. The Steyr Tactical Machine Pistol is exactly the same but has a front grip and can be switched to automatic fire, while this is a one-handed weapon which fires only in the semi-automatic mode.

Below: And this is the Heckler & Koch submission, which won the contract and provided the pistols.

Introduction

Rifles

Right and Below: SIG, in co-operation with the German company J. P. Sauer & Son, produce world-class target rifles — as this SIG-Sauer Model 205.

The development of the rifle in the 20th century has been an erratic affair, different areas having been driven by different imperatives. The advance of the sporting rifle has been largely driven by ammunition; sportsmen have demanded higher velocities, either for cleaner killing of bigger game or for greater accuracy on the target range. Ammunition makers (or private individuals — the so-called "wild-catters") have produced cartridges and rifle makers have modified their designs accordingly, making them stronger. But so far as the mechanical arrangements go there has been very little innovation; most of today's sporting rifles use a bolt mechanism which, essentially, is little changed from Mauser's design of 1898, while the popular lever-actions are even older. As with other types of weapon, manufacturing methods have changed considerably. Hand-built guns are still to be found — at a price — but modern machining techniques and modern materials can produce a well-finished, accurate, and reliable rifle in a fraction of the time and at a fraction of the cost. A good rifle is not cheap; but then, it never was. If you compare two rifles of comparable quality, one from the 1900s and one from the 1990s, and then compare their prices to the average man's income, it will generally be safe to say that today's rifle is cheaper in real terms. And it is also safe to say that if the development of rifles had been entirely dependent upon the sporting scene, then we would still be using much the same weapons as were in use in the 1900s.

If we look at military rifles, it is an entirely different story. Although popular legend tells us that it was military conservatism that delayed the arrival of the automatic rifle, that is not quite all the story. The military was not simply concerned with the prospect of the soldier shooting off all his ammunition in the first two minutes of combat, but more with ensuring that when the soldier did get an automatic rifle it would continue to operate in spite of the atrocious conditions to which it would be subjected. Automatic rifles appeared on the sporting scene before 1910, but what was acceptable to a hunter was not always acceptable to a soldier. If a hunter's rifle jammed at the wrong moment, he might miss his dinner; if a soldier's rifle did the same thing, his life was on the line. So the early specifications laid down by various armies all demanded absolute efficiency and backed it up by requiring that if the automatic mechanism failed, then the weapon must still be manually operable. As you might imagine, this led to some very complicated designs.

Another problem of the 1900s was the existence of patents. Suppose an inventor took out a patent on a rotating bolt; he might not have been able to make it work, but so long as he held that patent, nobody else was going to try and make it work either, because the patent

holder would have claimed his fee as soon as it did. This also led to some very complicated designs as people tried to work around patents. Once all these various basic patents expired, then inventors could begin making some simpler designs. Another brake on progress was that many inventors had not the slightest idea of what sort of forces were let loose inside a firearm when it fired. This led to weapons with astronomical rates of fire, violent recoil, separated cases, and every other defect and disaster that can be imagined. Gradually all these various points were studied and understood, some fundamental research was done, mathematical formulae were worked out, and eventually practical rifles appeared; rifles which were not too heavy for the soldier to carry all day, fired at an acceptable rate, didn't get too hot, didn't jam as soon as a speck of sand landed on the bolt, and didn't lose their accuracy as they warmed up. But it was the 1930s before the first of these appeared, and many armies preferred to let some more research take place — as well as a major war — before they eventually chose their automatic rifle in the 1950s.

The following pages detail the story of these rifles. Obviously, due to the space available, it has been impossible to list every rifle made in the past century, but the main thread of development has been closely followed. As to where we go next: current military thinking is towards some sort of double-barrelled weapon, one barrel firing a conventional bullet, the other firing some sort of explosive shell. Ceramics and synthetic materials, caseless cartridges, flechettes, and many other ideas are being thrown around. All that can be suggested is wait and see. But whatever the solution is, you can be sure of one thing; it won't be cheap.

A Century

Below Right: The Martini-Henry Cavalry Carbine used the classic Peabody-Martini lever action, lowering the forward edge of the breech block to permit the cartridges to be loaded. No longer in military use, the action survives in target rifles.

As the new century dawned, there were essentially five kinds of rifle: single-shot rifles, largely used for hunting and target shooting; double rifles — constructed in similar fashion to a side-by-side shotgun but with rifled barrels — for hunting big game; slide-action magazine rifles, largely confined to .22 caliber and used for hunting small game and target shooting; lever-action magazine rifles, also for hunting; and bolt action magazine rifles which were almost all for military service. By the middle of the century the list had expanded to include the automatic rifle, then in use by a number of armies. And, as the century draws to its close, every one of those types is still being manufactured though the proportions have changed — double rifles are much less common as the number of big game hunters has diminished and other types of rifle have gained in power, slide action rifles are less common as the more stringent laws relating to the ownership and use of firearms in general have struck hard against "fun guns" in Europe, and bolt action rifles are restricted to sniping in military circles — but the choice is still there.

The single shot rifle is today almost entirely found as a precision target weapon or as a replica of some older weapon, and the choice of breech actions is therefore limited. At the beginning of the century things were different and the single shot rifle was common, particularly in those parts of the world where it was still common practice to take a rifle and a handful of cartridges in the late afternoon and wander out, perhaps with a dog, to shoot supper. This type of owner, the farmer or homesteader, had no call for the capacity of a magazine rifle. A frugal man, he learned to shoot at an early age and learned to shoot well, so that one shot was usually as much as he required to fill the larder. The extras were there just in case of ill-luck or, in some places, as insurance against encountering an animal that was also looking for its supper.

Perhaps the single-shot mechanism that has survived longest is the Peabody-Martini, named for Peabody who invented the basic principle and Martini who perfected it. In this system the breech is closed by a steel block hinged at the rear end and moved, by a lever behind the trigger, so that the front end swings down to expose the chamber and permit a round to be loaded, and then swung up again so as to place the block solidly behind the cartridge. The block contains the firing pin and, due to the relatively small dimensions of the block, this has a short and rapid travel, leading to what is called a "short lock time" — the "lock time" being the time between pressing the trigger and starting the bullet up the bore; or between pressing the trigger and the bullet leaving the muzzle — definitions differ. But whichever way you prefer to define it, the result is the same: the lock time is the time between pressing the trigger and the effective commencement of the bullet's flight. And a short lock time obviously means less chance of the aim wandering off while the ignition of the cartridge is under way. Once the shot has been fired, the firer operates the lever, an extractor pulls the case out of the chamber and either ejects it or leaves it so exposed that the firer can flick it out of the way, and he can then reload.

The Martini action was still in military service at the turn of the century; not with first-line troops in any major army, but in reserves and with para-military forces such as border guards. It was certainly in service with the Suez Canal Police force as late as 1949 and it would not be surprising to find one or two of these rifles still in use in the wilder parts of the world today.

Most contemporary single shot rifle mechanisms, however, are either replicas or modernizations of the Remington falling block, another long-established system. This is exactly as the name implies, a block of steel sliding up and down in a mortice slot at the rear of the chamber, controlled by a lever beneath the trigger. On a larger scale, the same sort of mechanism closes the rear end of thousands of heavy artillery weapons, so that there is no lack of strength, allowing it to be a compact and efficient system for use with the most powerful sporting cartridges.

Although the single-shot rifle was common in the early years of the century it was losing ground. Most people buying rifles wanted a maga-zine weapon, something they could "load on Sunday and shoot for the rest of the week" as the American Civil War joke had it. And in the American civil market the lever-action rifle was far and away the popular choice. The Winchester had pioneered this type of weapon, in which a lever below and behind the trigger was pushed down to withdraw the bolt and open the chamber, ejecting any spent case. The final movement of the lever also operated a "cartridge lifter" which raised a cartridge from the tubular magazine beneath the barrel and positioned it in front of the

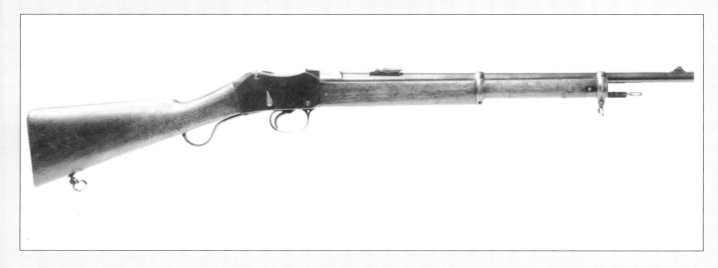

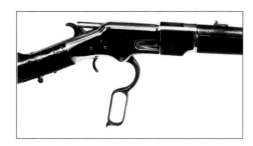

Above: A Winchester Model 66 carbine with the lever at full stretch, showing how the breech bolt cocks the hammer. The loading port can be seen just above the lever.

Below: The Winchester lever action rifle uses a tubular magazine beneath the barrel. Operating the lever cocks the hammer and moves a "cartridge lifter" to align a cartridge with the chamber. The upward stroke of the lever then rams the round and locks the breech, leaving the hammer cocked.

bolt. The return stroke of the lever forced the bolt forward, ramming the fresh cartridge into the chamber, then locked the bolt securely, leaving a hammer cocked ready to fire.

There were only two real drawbacks to the lever-action rifle; the cartridge needed to be of moderate length, otherwise the design became complicated if the bolt had to be withdrawn a long distance to permit loading a long cartridge; and the ammunition had to have soft-point or flat-tipped bullets, since the shock of firing was liable to cause the cartridges in the magazine to set back, and if a sensitive cap sat back on to a sharply pointed bullet, a magazine explosion could easily occur. These two reasons are why lever-action military rifles were rarely successful, and when you add the difficulty of operating a lever-action rifle while lying as close to the ground as possible in order to avoid being shot, you have a fairly comprehensive case against military lever-actions.

But for sporting use these were of little account and the popularity and reliability of the Winchester led to others entering the same field with slightly different designs (to avoid patent lawsuits) but of similar operation. Savage and Marlin entered the lever-action business, and, together with Winchester they are still in it, making a range of rifles which cover the

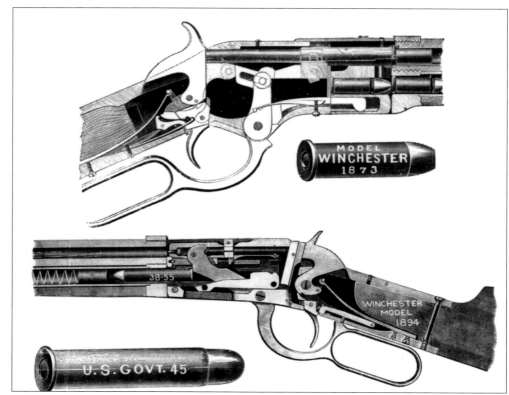

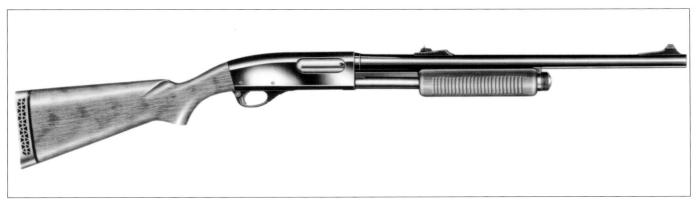

calibers from .22 rimfire to .45 Colt. For the most part they adhere to the rule of using moderate-length cartridges, but modern technology and careful design has allowed them to go so far as to use such cartridges as the 7.62mm NATO and .30-06 with complete reliability. The Savage Model 99C and the Browning BLR 81 are notable for using box magazines, which obviates the bullet-to-cap problem with pointed bullets, but the Winchester and Marlin range stick with the original type of tubular magazine, though they reduce the capacity for the military-style cartridges.

The slide action (or pump action) is still with us; but only just. Fifty years ago every fairground in Europe and the USA had a shooting gallery stocked with .22 rimfire slide-action rifles (usually with discreetly warped barrels and dubiously-set sights) with which many a youngster was introduced to the pleasures of shooting. Today, in Europe at any event, these rifles are fast becoming collector's items as repressive legislation has relegated the fairground shooting booth to a distant memory. A quick glance through current catalogs shows only one slide-action rifle still being made — the Remington 7600, available in calibers from .243 to .35 Whelen. This is a beautiful weapon, reasonably priced and worth buying because before very long it, too, will be a collector's piece.

In considering the bolt action, we really ought to begin with the military side of things, because in 1900 there were more bolt actions around than could possibly be imagined. Almost every country had its own design, and commercial bolt actions grew out of the military adoption.

Top: A Marlin carbine chambered for the .30-30 cartridge and with a five-shot tubular magazine.

Above: Pump actions are now becoming rare on rifles, but are still popular on shotguns, as shown by the Remington Model 870 deer gun.

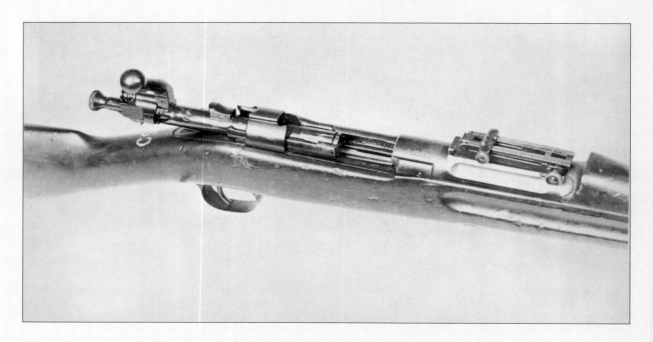

The bolt action, simple and obvious as it may seem to be, was born rather late in the history of firearms and was created to fill a military need. It first appeared on the Dreyse Needle Gun delivered to the Prussian Army in 1848, then on the French Chassepot of 1866 and the Swiss Vetterli of 1867, after which the designs flew thick and fast. The basic need was to open the rear end of the rifle, and close it securely so that it didn't blow open under the pressure of the exploding cartridge; this seemed simple enough to begin with, but as cartridges got more powerful, so the reliable locking of the bolt became more difficult, particularly as it was vital to make the operation of the bolt as simple and swift as possible. This became even more vital when the magazine rifle became practical, since the object now was to get off a series of shots as quickly as possible into the ranks of a charging enemy. Different inventors had different ideas of how to go about this, and, of course, their ideas were also conditioned by the need to avoid anything that had already been patented by somebody else.

In 1900, there were two types of bolt mechanism: the turn-bolt, which, as the name suggests, was opened and closed by lifting the handle so as to rotate the bolt, then pulling it back and pushing it forward, turning the handle down again to complete the locking; and the straight-pull bolt which, as you might guess, was operated by simply grasping the bolt handle, pulling it straight back and pushing it straight forward again; all the mysteries of locking and unlocking were done mechanically by the simple reciprocatory movement.

The turnbolt was locked in place by lugs on the bolt which, as the bolt handle was turned down, moved into engagement with recesses in either the barrel or the receiver, and at this point the turnbolt splits into two camps, front-locking and rear-locking. Rear-locking is the simplest of the two; a suitable slot is cut in the side of the rifle body (the receiver) and the handle turns down into it, so that any rearward movement of the bolt is prevented by the back of the handle pressing against the rear edge of the slot. This is fine so long as relatively weak cartridges are being fired (all early .22 rimfire bolt action rifles, for example, used this simple

system). As cartridges became more powerful so it became necessary for additional lugs to be put on the bolt, and recesses were also cut into the receiver on the opposite side to the handle. These modifications meant that the stress was more evenly distributed and the strain taken by more than one point. But the theoretical drawback to the rear-locking bolt was that with high-powered cartridges there was a compression of the body of the bolt between its face, where the pressure of the exploding cartridge was imposed, and the faces of the lugs and their recesses, and this compression tended to an unsteadiness in the cartridge and inaccuracy in the rifle.

The front-locking bolt didn't suffer from this; here the bolt had lugs right at its forward end, and recesses were cut into the rear face of the chamber. As the bolt was pushed right home so the lugs lined up with the recesses, and turning the bolt turned the lugs into the recesses to make a very positive lock. And since the lugs were right on the head of the bolt there was nothing between them and the bolt face to compress, so there was no unsteadiness on firing. But the front-locking bolt carries a penalty; by its very design the unlocking rotation has to be completed before the bolt can begin to open. In a rear-locking bolt, it is possible to taper, or curve, or round off the rear faces of the locking recesses so that while the bolt is still rotating it can also begin its rearward movement; and, conversely, it can begin to rotate into the locked position before it is completely closed.

There were, of course, designers who backed both horses by putting lugs on both ends of the bolt, but they rank as front-locking because the rear lug was usually there as a form of insurance in case the front lug failed — not that there are many recorded instances of any such accident. One such was the Krag-Jorgensen rifle used by the US Army in 1900. This had originated in Norway, was then adopted by Denmark, and then by the USA, and its most prominent feature was the magazine which was loaded from the side. A trap-door was opened and loose cartridges pushed into the magazine, after which the door was closed, and a spring attached to the door then pressed on the cartridges, pushing them under the bolt and

Above: A Norwegian Krag-Jorgensen carbine, showing the side trap-door into which cartridges were loaded.

76

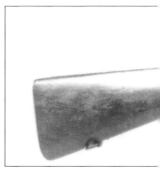

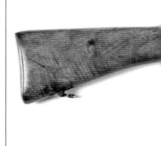

Top Right: The US Springfield M1903 rifle. Instead of a long rifle for infantry and a short carbine for cavalry and pioneers, the US and British armies both, in 1903, adopted a short rifle for everybody.

Middle Right: The Lee bolt and box magazine, seen here on a British Short Lee-Enfield rifle Mark III*.

Bottom Right: The German Mauser Gewehr 98 infantry rifle, a typical "long" rifle. It remained in use until World War I but was then gradually replaced by various short rifle designs.

up so as to feed into the action from the left side. An advantage was that the door could be opened and loose cartridges dropped in to top up the magazine at any time. The rifle was serviceable enough — the Norwegians and Danes continued to use it until the late 1940s and many are still in use in Scandinavia as hunting rifles — but the Americans used it in the Spanish-American War and came up against the German Mauser rifle in the hands of the Spaniards. This appeared to be of superior accuracy and striking power, and so by 1900 the US Army was testing Mauser rifles and, in 1903, adopted a Mauser design, calling it the Springfield rifle after the armory that had developed it.

The Mauser bolt action is, by any measure, the standard with which all others are compared. It uses two front locking lugs, reinforced by a third rear lug, and has proved strong enough to withstand any loading you care to think of. The magazine holds five rounds, is a box concealed within the stock of the rifle, and is loaded by a charger or "stripper clip" inserted into the top of the open action and holding five cartridges. These are swept from the charger and into the magazine by thumb pressure; closing the bolt flicks the charger out of the way and loads the first cartridge. The Mauser was, of course, the standard rifle of the German Army, but it was also adopted by armies of nations all over the world.

The British Army adopted the Lee bolt and magazine. This was a rear-locking bolt, and the magazine was a removable box beneath the stock which held, in its final form, ten rounds loaded from two five-round chargers. While theoretically not so accurate as the Mauser bolt, and less strong, it was nevertheless the fastest military bolt action ever made and pre-1914 trained soldiers were expected to be able to fire 30 aimed rounds per minute, something impossible with any front-locking turnbolt.

Other turnbolt actions generally owed something to the Mauser but differed in minor details. The only one to show great originality was the Austrian Mannlicher rifle used by the Greek Army. This had locking lugs towards the front of the bolt, but set back behind the bolt head, and had a rotary magazine. This was loaded from the usual stripper clip and rotated as the cartridges were pushed in, winding up a spring. As the rounds were fired, so the spring rotated the spool and presented each fresh cartridge to the bolt. This rifle stayed in service until 1945.

Straight-pull bolts were used by Austria (another Mannlicher design), by the Swiss, and by the Canadians. Mannlicher had two ways of making straight-pull bolts work; his first had a swinging block beneath the bolt which, as the bolt was pushed home, was forced down in front of a recess in the receiver behind the magazine. This proved to be serviceable but not sufficiently strong to withstand long use, and it was replaced by a system in which the bolt handle was attached to a hollow tube that fitted around the actual bolt. The bolt had lugs on its front and two spiral

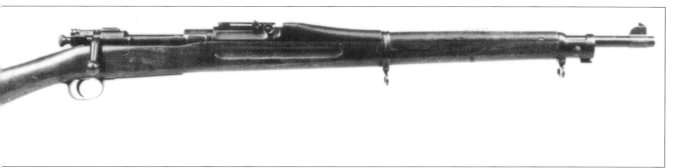

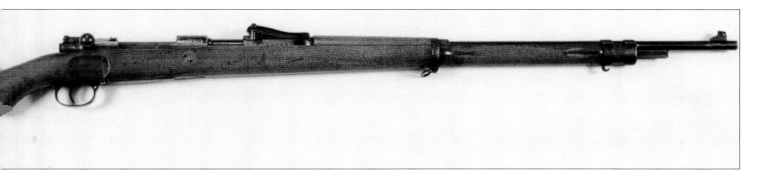

grooves on its rear end. The sleeve had two lugs on its inner surface which engaged the grooves in the bolt body. So that when the user pulled back on the handle he pulled the sleeve back; the lugs forced the grooves on the rear end of the bolt to conform with their path and thus the bolt body was rotated and unlocked the front lugs from the front end of the receiver. As the locking lugs disengaged, so the lugs and grooves came to the end of their run and the bolt was drawn open as the sleeve continued backwards.

The Swiss Schmidt-Rubin straight-pull bolt used a cam system but arranged it differently. The handle was attached to a rod lying alongside the bolt carrying a lug engaged in a spiral groove in the bolt body. Pulling back the handle drew the lug through the grooves, rotating and then opening the bolt in much the same way as the Mannlicher system. The Canadian Ross used a system similar to the Mannlicher, but less well thought out; it was possible to assemble it incorrectly and still fire it, whereupon, if the user was unlucky, the bolt blew straight out of the rear of the rifle.

In 1900, there was a distinct difference between the weapons issued to the infantry soldier and the remainder of any army — the cavalry and

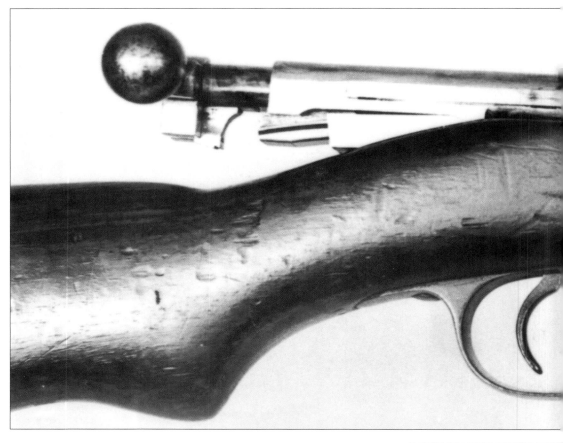

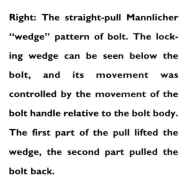

Right: The straight-pull Mannlicher "wedge" pattern of bolt. The locking wedge can be seen below the bolt, and its movement was controlled by the movement of the bolt handle relative to the bolt body. The first part of the pull lifted the wedge, the second part pulled the bolt back.

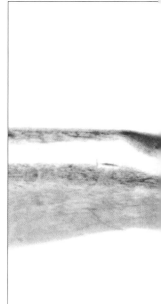

artillery carried short carbines, while the infantryman carried a long rifle. They both fired the same ammunition, but this system meant two supply systems for spares and replacement, and, with modern ammunition, there was little point in it. So, in 1903, the British broke new ground by providing all their army with the same weapon — a "short rifle;" shorter than the standard infantry rifle but longer than the normal carbine. The Short Magazine Lee-Enfield Mark III rifle became the standard weapon, and, after it had proved itself in World War I, a slightly different version, designed to be easier to mass-produce, became the "Rifle No. 4" that fought World War II.

The short rifle idea was soon copied; the American Springfield was the next to appear, followed by the Mauser Karabiner 98, a shortened version of their standard 1898 rifle. But the Germans had another surprise up their sleeve; the pointed bullet. Until 1905, the standard military rifle bullet was round-nosed and parallel-walled, with a square-cut base. The core was of lead, and the jacket of gilded metal or steel. This worked well and everybody was happy. But then spark photography (the 1900s version of the electronic flash) was invented and somebody thought it would be interesting to try and photograph a bullet in flight. It worked; and not only did it show the bullet but it also showed the compression and rarification of the air through which the bullet was passing, and some ballisticians began to realize that perhaps the bullet shape wasn't so good after all. The round nose appeared to build up a serious compression wave in front that caused the bullet to expend energy in pushing its way through. Experiments showed that a pointed bullet reduced this standing wave and folded it back, offering less

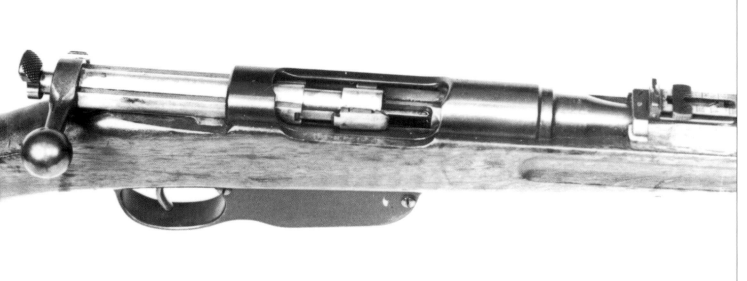

Above: The "sleeve" pattern of a Mannlicher straight-pull bolt; the handle is attached to a sleeve around the bolt, and a cam track inside the sleeve rotates the bolt at the appropriate time..

Right: The Mexican Mondragon rifle. The Mexican Army models used a box magazine; the drum magazine seen here was a German addition when the rifles were issued to the early aviators for self-defense.

obstruction. So, in 1905, the "Spitzer" (pointed) bullet appeared for the Mauser rifle, and in no time at all the armies of the world were changing over to pointed bullets and having to fit their rifles with new sights to take advantage of the higher velocity and longer range.

Ever since 1884, when Hiram Maxim had shown that an automatic machine gun was a practical proposition, inventors had been toying with the idea of making the infantryman's rifle automatic; or, more precisely, semi-automatic — a rifle that would fire and then reload itself without the soldier having to do anything. The army officers of the world were less sure about this idea. Give a soldier a rifle he didn't have to re-load and he would shoot off everything in the magazine while the enemy were still 1,000 meters away and then have no ammunition left when they got close in. And what if this complicated mechanism broke down just at the crucial moment as the enemy formed up for the final charge? So every army laid down a set of specifications that any automatic or semi-automatic rifle had to meet before any inventor could manufacture these weapons, and they were usually so stringent that a lot of the military rifles in service in 1995 would have had trouble meeting them. Some of them, dealing with weight and size and balance were eminently sensible; some, such as the universal demand that if the mechanism failed then the weapon should be operable as a manual loader, merely added complication to already difficult mechanisms. It must also be remembered that in those days almost every conceivable method of operating a firearm had been patented by somebody and an inventor had to be very wary that they didn't work on some other patentee's design in their search for a workable gun. Complication was almost guaranteed!

Nevertheless, a few inventors got in with a chance. The Danish Marines took an automatic rifle in the mid-1890s; though only a few, and these were not wildly successful. However, the inventor went away and modified it before re-introducing it as the Madsen light machine gun, a success story in its own right. Others tried; Mauser produced several designs, as did Mannlicher, but the first one to actually get into military service in the 20th century came from an unexpected quarter — Mexico.

Mexico had no arms industry, and bought all its weapons abroad; the army used Mauser rifles and Krupp cannon. But General Mondragon of the Mexican Army was a small arms expert and he worked for several years on an automatic rifle design which he eventually had manufactured by the Swiss Industrial Company (today better-known as SIG) and the first were issued to the Mexican Army in 1908.

The Mondragon rifle used a gas piston working in a cylinder beneath the barrel; a portion of the gas pushing the bullet was diverted into the cylinder and forced back the piston. A stud on the rear end of the piston rod connected with the bolt by means of a curved groove, so that as the

piston went back so it rotated the bolt to unlock it, and then opened it to eject the spent case. A spring then drove the piston rod forward again, closing the bolt and loading the next round. A locking catch on the bolt handle allowed the piston to be disconnected and the rifle then worked like a straight-pull bolt action; this being the requisite manual fall-back if the gas system failed for any reason.

Like everything from SIG it was beautifully made of the finest materials and must have been expensive for its day. It fired a 7mm Mauser cartridge, the standard Spanish pattern used all over Central and South America, though promotional models were also made by SIG in other calibers. The last of the order was still being made when war descended in August 1914; SIG were unable to get them to Mexico and they were bought by Germany who used them first to arm infantrymen but, finding that the mud and dirt of ground fighting tended not to agree with the Mondragon mechanism, withdrew them and gave them to aviators for the first tentative attempts at aerial combat in 1914/15.

This experience of the Germans with an automatic rifle in the mud of Flanders merely seemed to confirm what everybody suspected about these sensitive weapons and little more was heard about them during the war years. Mauser produced a fresh design in 1915, but this, after some cursory trials in the trenches, also went to the fledgling air force. In Russia, an engineer named Vasilly Federov had been working on a design since 1908, but he approached things from a slightly different angle. His first thought was that the contemporary rifle cartridge was far too powerful, and led to a heavy and cumbersome weapon. So he designed his rifle around the small 6.5mm Japanese service cartridge, stocks of which had been captured by the Russians in the Russo-Japanese War in 1904. Federov was happy to accept the lower performance for the advantage of a lighter and less stressed weapon. It says a lot for the Tsarist army that

Above: The Browning Automatic Rifle — the BAR — was pushed into rapid production in 1917 to allow the U.S. troops to take it to Germany when they entered the war. In fact it was the U.S. Army's 79th Division that used it first in action, in September 1918. It was manufactured by Winchester (Above), Colt (Top), and Rockwell and would see service in World War II as the U.S. infantry squad support weapon.

they were willing to listen and willing to put the "Federov Automat" into production in 1916, even though it demanded a special supply of ammunition. But the Revolution came along before much experience had been gained (and before many people outside the Tsar's army knew of the existence of the weapon). Remarkably, the new masters also saw the sense of the Automat and put it back into production. About 9,000 were made before production ended in 1924, and thus while the world's armies discussed the future of the automatic rifle, largely unknown to them there were several thousand Russian soldiers who were using one every day.

There was also a French design, the St Etienne, which appeared in 1917. This fired the 8mm Lebel rifle cartridge, which was powerful but awkwardly shaped for automatic feed and had to be loaded with a special clip. The whole rifle was long, ungainly and prone to jams. A lighter model, capable of using the regulation clip of ammunition as used with

Left: John C. Garand (1887–1974), inventor of the Garand M1 rifle. Born in Canada, he went to the USA at an early age and became a US citizen in 1912. During World War I he designed a machine gun and offered it to the US Army. They were impressed and he was later invited to work as a designer at Springfield Armory. He developed the M1 rifle and remained there until he retired in 1953.

Above: The long and cumbersome St Etienne automatic rifle of 1917, issued in some numbers to the French army but soon withdrawn as it failed to withstand the rigors of the front line.

bolt-action rifles, appeared in 1918, but it was little better, and eventually those that survived the war were converted to manual operation and given to various colonial troops.

Consequently, after the war there was a reasonable body of experience with the automatic rifle and what could be expected of it in combat; the problem was to design out the various defects which had appeared, and there was no shortage of inventors willing to try. Of them, two stand out — Pedersen and Garand. Pedersen was an engineer who had worked for Remington until 1917, when he had gone to the US arsenal at Springfield. After the war he began designing an automatic rifle using a toggle-joint breech lock similar to that of the Parabellum (Luger) pistol but proportioned so as to act as a delayed blowback mechanism. The cam surfaces in the toggle were so designed as to resist the breech pressure initially and then slowly unfold the two limbs of the toggle so as to extract the spent case. The folding action then accelerated to eject the

Top Right: The Pedersen T2 rifle with its breech locking toggle open. Had it not been for the need for lubricated ammunition, this might well have become the US Army's rifle instead of the Garand.

Middle Right: The M1 Garand rifle, complete with bayonet. Gas-operated, it had an eight-round magazine which was loaded by a clip.

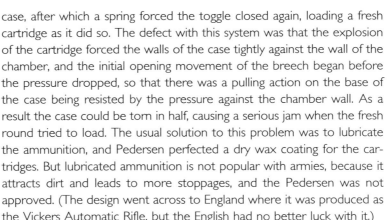

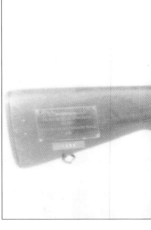

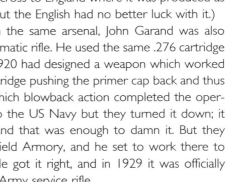

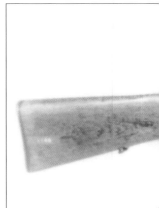

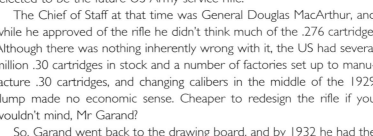

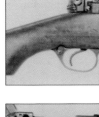

case, after which a spring forced the toggle closed again, loading a fresh cartridge as it did so. The defect with this system was that the explosion of the cartridge forced the walls of the case tightly against the wall of the chamber, and the initial opening movement of the breech began before the pressure dropped, so that there was a pulling action on the base of the case being resisted by the pressure against the chamber wall. As a result the case could be torn in half, causing a serious jam when the fresh round tried to load. The usual solution to this problem was to lubricate the ammunition, and Pedersen perfected a dry wax coating for the cartridges. But lubricated ammunition is not popular with armies, because it attracts dirt and leads to more stoppages, and the Pedersen was not approved. (The design went across to England where it was produced as the Vickers Automatic Rifle, but the English had no better luck with it.)

At the same time, and in the same arsenal, John Garand was also working on his idea of an automatic rifle. He used the same .276 cartridge that Pedersen used, and by 1920 had designed a weapon which worked by the gas pressure in the cartridge pushing the primer cap back and thus unlocking the breech, after which blowback action completed the operating cycle. This he offered to the US Navy but they turned it down; it needed special ammunition and that was enough to damn it. But they offered him a post at Springfield Armory, and he set to work there to design a gas-operated rifle. He got it right, and in 1929 it was officially selected to be the future US Army service rifle.

The Chief of Staff at that time was General Douglas MacArthur, and while he approved of the rifle he didn't think much of the .276 cartridge. Although there was nothing inherently wrong with it, the US had several million .30 cartridges in stock and a number of factories set up to manufacture .30 cartridges, and changing calibers in the middle of the 1929 slump made no economic sense. Cheaper to redesign the rifle if you wouldn't mind, Mr Garand?

So, Garand went back to the drawing board, and by 1932 he had the .30 caliber version working — it was standardized as the "Rifle, US, Cal .30 M1." Due to lack of money, manufacture did not begin until 1936, but even with that delay the US Army was still the first army in the world to adopt a semi-automatic rifle as the infantryman's standard weapon.

By this time, the middle 1930s, similar work was going on in Europe. The Soviet Army had decided on an automatic rifle for its troops, and several design teams were set to work. Two were selected, one by Simonov, the other by Tokarev, both of whom were well-respected weapon designers. Simonov had begun his work by helping Fedorov develop the Automat, and in 1932 he began work on a rifle of his own, which went into service in 1936 as the AVS-36. It was gas operated, fired single shots or automatic fire, and locked the bolt by a vertically-moving

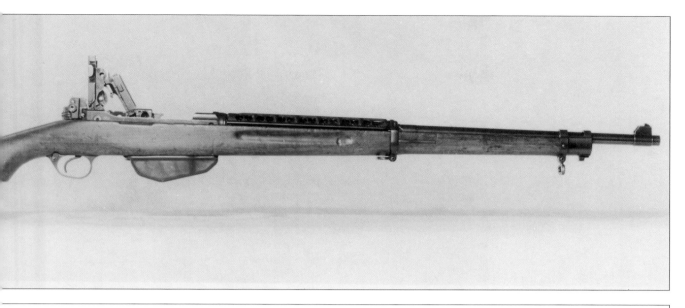

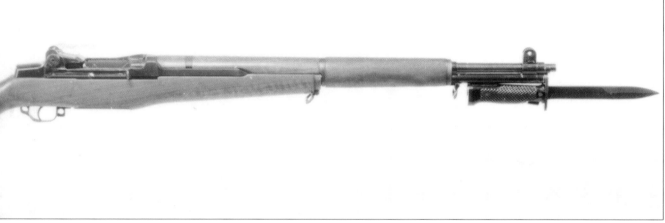

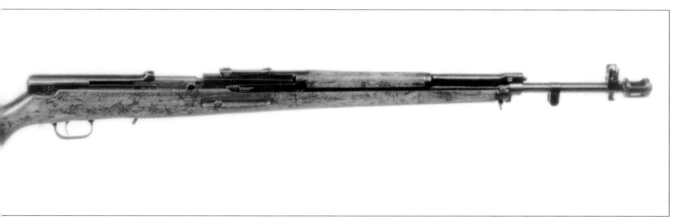

block, but it suffered from excessive muzzle blast and needed a muzzle brake to make it acceptable. However, practical use showed that it was not capable of standing up to the rigors of military life and by 1938 the rifle was withdrawn.

Tokarev spent the 1920s developing machine guns, then produced the automatic pistol that became the Soviet standard weapon, after which he began work on a gas-operated rifle which became the SVT-38 and

Above: The Russian Simonov SVT36, a gas operated automatic rifle using the Russian 7.62mm rimmed cartridge. Note the prominent muzzle brake, an attempt to reduce the recoil force on the firer's shoulder.

Top right: The Russian Tokarev automatic rifle of 1938, the SVT-38. Like the Simonov design it needed a muzzle brake to reduce the kick, and, also like the Simonov, it was hard for the designers to break away from the traditional shape of a rifle.

replaced the defective Simonov. It, too, proved to be too fragile for service. He was able to produce a strengthened version, the SVT-40, but even this was thought to be too delicate for the rough-and-tumble of infantry combat and it became a specialist sniper weapon.

The principal problem with both these rifles was that they were built around the old 7.62mm rimmed cartridge that had been developed in 1895 for the Mosin-Nagant bolt-action rifle. Like all cartridges of that era it was designed to go a long way and still be effective, and that meant it was a powerful round, really too powerful to be fired from the shoulder in an automatic weapon.

This problem of using very powerful cartridges was the problem that all designers of automatic rifles encountered at that time; Garand's achievement was not so much that he designed a rifle but that he designed one which fired the .30-06, one of the most powerful of military cartridges, and made it work reliably. The Germans, faced with designing a rifle around the 7.92mm Mauser cartridge, of roughly the same potency, decided to approach the problem from a different direction.

In the mid-1930s a group of German officers were given the task of planning a new infantry rifle, and in order to do so they began by asking some very basic questions, like "Just what is the soldier expected to do with a rifle?" They interrogated soldiers who had fought in 1914–18, contemplated the course of warfare, and came up with some new and provocative conclusions. In the first place, they said, we currently have an infantry rifle firing a heavy cartridge capable of ranging to 2,000 meters or more. How many times does a soldier actually fire his rifle at that sort of range? More to the point, how many times can a soldier even see a target at that range? And by "target" they meant not the usual six-foot square of white paper, but a real living man, dressed in field gray or green, hiding in the hedgerows. These and similar questions led to the discovery that very few soldiers had, in combat, ever fired at ranges more than 400 or 500 meters. The terrain rarely gave them a clear shot at greater ranges, and anyway it was hard to pick up a living target at more than 500 meters. So, the officers determined, what we really need is a smaller, less powerful cartridge which will be satisfactory to 600 or 800 meters; longer ranges can be left to machine guns. And if you have a smaller and less powerful cartridge you can have a shorter and lighter rifle; so that for a given weight the soldier can carry his rifle and a larger amount of ammunition.

As a result of this reasoning, a 7mm short cartridge was designed which promised to provide all the performance that was needed in a suitably small package. (As an aside, it is remarkable that whenever experts gather to decide on a new caliber they almost always end up recommending 7mm as the ideal caliber.) However, it was 1939, the war

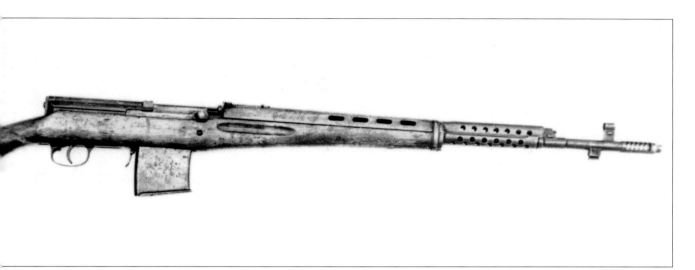

was just commencing, and there was no way that anybody in Germany was going to suggest a complete change of caliber; like the Americans in 1932, they had too much invested in 7.92mm ammunition stocks and manufacturing plants. So the officers thought again and changed the design into a 7.92mm short cartridge, so that as much as possible could be made of existing machinery. (Another aside: although 7mm has often been recommended, it has never been adopted by any major army.)

With a cartridge designed they then turned to the gunmakers and asked for a suitable selective-fire rifle — a rifle that would provide single shots or automatic fire at choice, and one which could be rapidly mass-produced. The Haenel and Walther companies took up the challenge and in 1942 produced prototypes. Several thousand of each were made and sent to the German Army on the Eastern front for combat evaluation, as a result of which the Haenel design was selected for mass production. Then politics came into the picture.

The Maschinen Karabiner 42(H) was a gas-operated rifle capable of firing 500 shots a minute; it fired the new 7.92mm Short cartridge; it was reliable and it was well-liked by those who had used it. But when approval

Above: The designers of the German MP-44 had no reservations about breaking away from the traditional shapes and materials. The MP-44 assault rifle used no wood, was largely of stamped steel, and had a high-set plastic butt so as to reduce the lifting movement of the muzzle when fired. It didn't need a muzzle brake, since it fired a short 7.92mm cartridge.

Above: The MP-44 was the weapon selected to use the "Krummlauf" attachment that allowed the rifle to be fired round corners with the aid of a bulky mirror sight.

Right: "So this is what they're using. . ." A British general gets the feel of the German assault rifle, examining a collection of captured weapons in the winter of 1944.

to manufacture was sought, Adolf Hitler vetoed it. He had served on the Western front during the last war and he knew that rifles had to shoot 2,000 meters or they weren't rifles. So no production. The soldiers, as soldiers do, saluted, fell out. . . and went ahead with their production plans. But they changed the weapon's name to "Maschinen Pistole 43" so that it showed in the production returns for sub-machine guns. And since Adolf Hitler was keen on submachine guns he was quite pleased to see that production in that department was rising.

Of course, the deception couldn't last for ever. A conference of commanders from the Eastern Front was called, and when Hitler asked if there was anything they needed, he was taken aback when they all demanded more of the new rifle. He was even more surprised when he discovered that his personal bodyguard were all armed with the new weapon. The uproar died down eventually, and Hitler relented far enough to bestow a third name on the weapon; he called it the Sturmgewehr 44 or "assault rifle," and although he never knew it he had called an entire new generation of weapons into existence.

The Sturmgewehr was not the only automatic rifle which had appeared in Germany. The paratroop element of the German forces was part of the Luftwaffe (Air Force) and not the army; and when the army were developing the Sturmgewehr the paratroops looked at it but turned it down; the cartridge was too small, they said, in our particular tactical situation we need the extra range and hitting power of the full sized 7.92mm cartridge, so we want a selective-fire rifle capable of using it. The Army replied that they had looked at all this and reached the conclusion that such a weapon was out of the question. So the paratroops went to

the top of their own chain of command and persuaded Marshal Herman Goering, chief of the Luftwaffe, to back them. They then went to Rheinmetall and Krieghoff, two premier gunmakers, and asked for the impossible.

Rheinmetall produced the answer, though since they had no spare capacity the gun was produced by Krieghoff. The Fallschirmgewehr 42 (Parachutist's Rifle 1942) was a technical triumph, a gas-operated, selective-fire rifle light enough to be easily carried but powerful enough to deliver the heavy 7.92mm bullet at 800 rounds per minute. However, by the time it was perfected and put into production the German paratroops had suffered severe casualties in Crete and saw very little airborne service thereafter, being largely used as foot infantry, and only about 7,000 rifles were manufactured.

One other German wartime development might be mentioned here, since it has a connection with rifle technology. In 1903, a German named Karl Puff patented an idea for making a firearm with a tapering bore, together with a bullet with a hard core and malleable metal "skirts" so

Below: The US Carbine M1, a rifle that fired a pistol bullet and intended to be a suitable self-defence weapon for non-infantry soldiers, a simple weapon, easily carried, and with more range than a pistol.

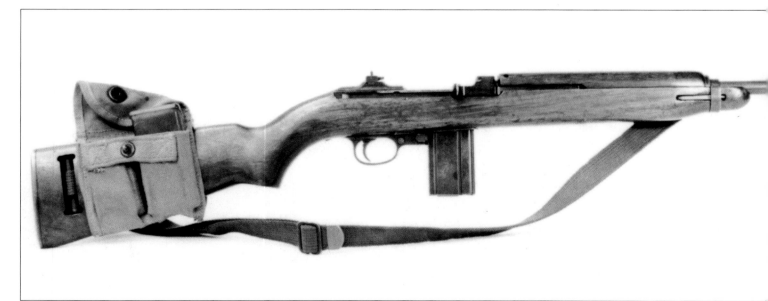

Left: They said it couldn't be done . . . The Fallschirmgewehr (Parachutist's rifle) 42 fired from the shoulder at full automatic with the powerful 7.92mm Mauser cartridge. A brilliant technical achievement for its day, it arrived just as the German parachute regiments were downgraded to ordinary infantry status, and as a result relatively few of these special rifles were made.

that it would gradually reduce in diameter, the skirts being squeezed down, as it passed from breech to muzzle. The advantage in this complication was that since the pressure of gas behind the bullet remained reasonably constant once all the powder had exploded, the reducing area of the base of the bullet meant an increased pressure per square centimeter and hence an increase in velocity. Everybody agreed it was a fine theory but the actual business of boring a tapered hole and rifling it, and making the somewhat complicated bullet, defeated the technology of the day. In the 1920s, though, an engineer named Gerlich and a gunsmith called Halbe got together and proceeded to make the idea work, calling the result the "Halger" rifle. They produced a few weapons, purchased by big game hunters who demanded high velocity for its benefits of a flat trajectory and killing power, after which Gerlich set out to try and interest armies in the idea, suggesting that it could make a valuable sniping weapon. He tried the British and American war departments, spending some time in Britain and the USA promoting his ideas and working on

Below: In spite of its ballistic shortcomings, soldiers liked the carbine because it was light and handy; here it is in the hands of a US Marine landing on Iwojima in February 1945.

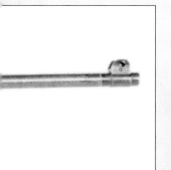

Right: Here a GI uses the oldest trick in the book to tempt a German out of concealment so that his partner with a carbine can shoot him. A scene in Normandy, during the summer of 1944.

experimental designs, but the general opinion was that while the idea worked, it was far too expensive for something as inherently simple as a bolt-action rifle. So Gerlich returned to Germany in the mid-1930s when the German Army was beginning to re-arm and interested the Rheinmetall company in his ideas, as a result of which the German Army eventually received three taper-bored anti-tank guns, one of 28mm tapering to 20mm, one of 42/29mm and one of 75/55mm. All three were phenomenally successful, but unfortunately their ammunition demanded the use of tungsten. This became too scarce to squander on throwing at an enemy and was confined to use in machine tools in 1942, so the Gerlich guns were phased out as their ammunition was expended. And although firearms ideas tend to come round in cycles, the taper bore is one which has never re-appeared in small calibers, though experimental artillery pieces continued to be made in various countries until the 1950s.

To return to the automatic rifle, the next interesting development came from the USA, when the army decided that it needed a self-defence weapon to replace the pistol in the hands of cooks, bakers, drivers, signalers, engineers, and all those many thousands of soldiers whose prime task was not shooting directly at their opposite numbers. A "light rifle" was what they asked for, and, in 1940, a special .30 cartridge was developed and several companies were asked to produce a suitable weapon. Nine weapons were submitted for evaluation by various companies, five of which were selected for further development, and, in September 1941, the Winchester design was selected to become the US Carbine .30 M1.

There is a legend, fostered by a James Stewart movie, that "Carbine" Williams of Winchester designed the carbine in ten days, but this is far from the truth. Early in 1940 Winchester developed a full-sized .30 automatic rifle using a short-stroke gas piston designed by Williams; this had been tried by the US and British but rejected as being insufficiently developed. At much the same time two employees of Winchester were, in their spare time, working on a light hunting rifle using the same short-stroke gas piston system of operation. Their activity had the firm's blessing, and when the army's demand for a light rifle appeared, Mr Pugsley, the Winchester chief engineer, called on the two men to make some changes in their design to suit the military requirements and see if they could make it work. Since their rifle was complete, the necessary changes were relatively easy, and thus Winchester were able to go into the contest with a design which already had most of the problems found and cured. Beyond the adoption of his gas piston, Williams had nothing whatsoever to do with the design of the carbine, Hollywood notwithstanding. (This information came from a number of old Winchester employees who were involved in the work at the time.)

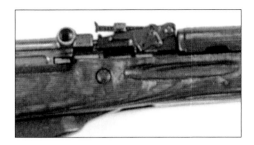

Above: The first Russian weapon to fire the 7.62 x 39mm short cartridge was this Simonov SKS-45 carbine. The bayonet was part of the rifle, and folded back under the barrel when not required.

The short-stroke piston demands a little explanation. The normal gas piston system of operating an automatic or self-loading weapon uses a gas cylinder attached to the barrel by a small port and containing a piston. Some of the gas behind the bullet goes through the port and drives the piston backwards to open the breech and reload, and the distance traveled by the piston is something rather more than the length of a complete cartridge. But in the Williams system the gas port leads to a small hollow block beneath the barrel, inside which is a flat-headed piston with a stem barely half an inch long protruding through the back of the block. Pressed against this block by a spring is the operating rod connected to the bolt. When the gas behind the bullet goes through the port in this design it drives the tiny piston back very forcefully, since the piston weighs no more than a couple of ounces. The protruding stem gives the operating rod a sharp blow, and the momentum so imparted to the rod is sufficient to drive it back and complete the reloading cycle. The system is light, simple, and easy to manufacture, which makes it all the more surprising that few other designs have ever adopted it.

Approximately 6.25 million carbines of various models (M1 — semi-automatic, M2 — selective fire, and M3 — fitted for infra-red sights) were made between 1941–45 and 1952–55, and from the 1960s onward a number of smaller companies began making replicas for the commercial market. Although the carbine fires what amounts to a pistol bullet and has limited range, it has proved a very popular weapon, largely because of its size and handiness; unfortunately this led many soldiers to adopt it in preference to their standard rifle, soldiers who then complained when it failed to perform adequately at 400 meters and longer ranges. But for self-defence and short range work the carbine remains a sound choice.

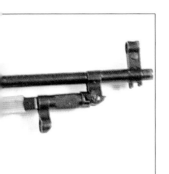

The appearance of the assault rifle in German hands on the Eastern front was followed, not surprisingly, by several of these weapons falling into the hands of Soviet troops. The Soviets examined them with great interest, and took even more interest in the cartridge, for they had been making experiments into short cartridges before the war began. Now able to see concrete evidence of their theories, they revived their research and eventually developed a 7.62mm short cartridge with good ballistic properties. They then turned to Simonov, the designer, and suggested that he develop an automatic rifle to suit. Simonov, by this time, had sufficient reports on his 1936 design to be able to improve on it, and in 1941 he had submitted a new rifle for test. It was considered a suitable design, but 1941 was no time for changing armament and the idea was put to one side. Now he brought it out again, redesigned it to suit the new cartridge, and by the summer of 1944 pre-production models were in the hands of troops on the Byelorussian front for practical testing in combat. This revealed sensitivity to dust and dirt, leading to jamming, and problems with extraction of the fired case. Simonov set to work and resolved these problems, and in the summer of 1945 his design was approved for issue as the SKS-45 carbine. Its appearance was traditional; a fully-wooden-stocked weapon with a folding bayonet underneath the fore-end and a fixed magazine holding ten rounds, loaded by means of a charger. It became the standard Soviet rifle and was later to be copied and manufactured in China, and to this day it can be seen in the hands of Russian troops on ceremonial duties.

Behind the scenes, however, another designer was at work in Russia, an unknown in 1944, but whose name was to become familiar throughout the world; Mikhail Timofeyevich Kalashnikov. Born in 1919, he was

Below: The rifle everyone recognizes: the Kalashnikov AK47 in its original form with wooden butt and fore-end grip.

Right: The AKS47 was the same weapon but with a folding metal butt.

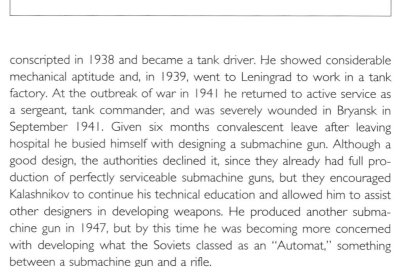

Right and Far Right: Other nations adopted the Kalashnikov; this is the Chinese "Type 56" rifle. The only difference is that there is a folding bayonet attached underneath the barrel.

Far Right Below: This variant of the Kalashnikov was made in East Germany and can be identified by the plastic butt and the projecting muzzle compensator which tries to keep the muzzle from rising when firing automatic.

conscripted in 1938 and became a tank driver. He showed considerable mechanical aptitude and, in 1939, went to Leningrad to work in a tank factory. At the outbreak of war in 1941 he returned to active service as a sergeant, tank commander, and was severely wounded in Bryansk in September 1941. Given six months convalescent leave after leaving hospital he busied himself with designing a submachine gun. Although a good design, the authorities declined it, since they already had full production of perfectly serviceable submachine guns, but they encouraged Kalashnikov to continue his technical education and allowed him to assist other designers in developing weapons. He produced another submachine gun in 1947, but by this time he was becoming more concerned with developing what the Soviets classed as an "Automat," something between a submachine gun and a rifle.

In 1946, Kalashnikov submitted drawings of his proposed design to the authorities; they responded by ordering prototypes to be made and tested. This was done, and some minor design flaws were sorted out by Kalashnikov and his team of assistants. In 1949, the weapon was approved

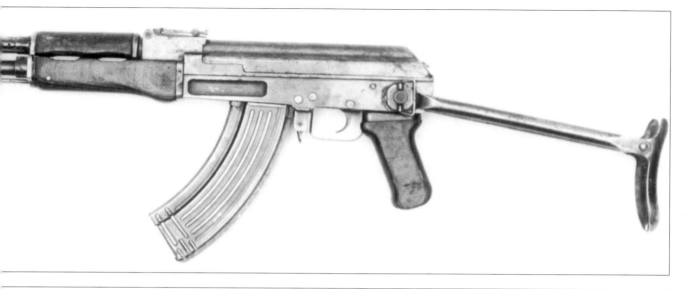

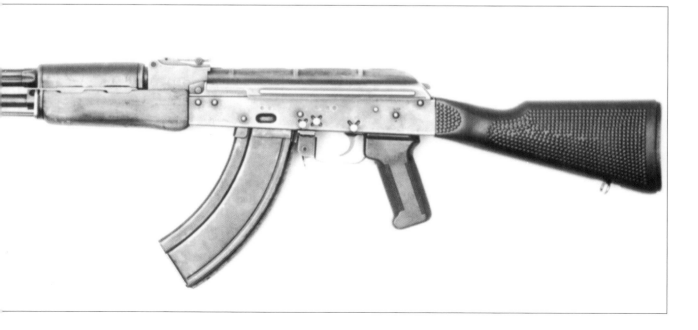

Below: The first that the West knew about the Russian AK47 5.45mm caliber rifle was this picture taken during a ceremonial parade in Moscow in 1980. The large muzzle brake indicated that here was something new but it was to be a year or two before everything was known.

for issue as the Automat Kalashnikov (AK) 47. Estimates vary, since no official figures have ever been compiled or are ever likely to be, but it is probable that since that day something more than 30 million Kalashnikov-pattern rifles have been made in various parts of the world, and there is probably no country in which it has not made an appearance.

What is the magic of the Kalashnikov? There isn't any; it is simply a good, robust, reliable, simple design. A target rifle it will never be; above 500 meters accuracy falls away rapidly. But as a tough combat weapon to put into the hands of ignorant conscripts, it is just about the ideal. Add to that, of course, the political policies of the Soviet Union, who were liberal in their gifts of weapons to anyone who looked like upsetting any non-Communist regime, coupled with their massive production facilities which ensured that these weapons could be mass-produced at rock-bottom cost, and the success of the Kalashnikov explains itself.

The AK 47 has a robust and simple mechanism. A gas cylinder above the barrel carries inside it a gas piston which is driven back by the propellant gas. The piston rod extends back into the receiver and becomes the bolt carrier, the bolt fitting into its underside. Behind the carrier is a guide rod and a return spring. As the gas drives the piston back, so the

bolt carrier moves back and a cam track cut into the carrier engages with a lug on the bolt to turn the bolt and unlock it from the chamber. This turning movement also has a slight rearward movement as the bolt comes to its unlocked position, so as to ease the cartridge from its seating in the chamber. Then the shape of the cam changes and the carrier now pulls the bolt back, opening the chamber and ejecting the spent case. This rearward movement has compressed the spring, and the bolt carrier has also over-ridden the firing hammer and re-cocked it. Now the spring re-asserts itself, drives the carrier forward, and the bolt collects a fresh cartridge from the 30-shot magazine and loads it into the chamber. The final forward movement of the carrier causes the cam track to rotate the bolt once more and lock it, and this movement also removes an intercepting surface that would otherwise prevent the hammer striking the firing pin should the bolt not lock properly. By operating a selector lever on the right side, the soldier can select single shots or automatic fire, when a rate of 600 rounds per minute is available.

The original AK 47 used a fully-machined receiver and was somewhat expensive to make, but in 1950 a "modernized" version, the AKM, was put into production. This used stamped metal and light alloy in various components to speed production and reduce weight, and it also

Above: The Russian invasion of Afghanistan resulted in the West learning a lot more about Russian weapons. Here an Afghan guerrilla demonstrates an AK47 rifle complete with a grenade launcher fitted beneath the barrel.

Above: The British 7mm EM2 rifle, the first "bullpup" design to be accepted for military use. Note how the breech goes all the way back to the shoulder pad, and the magazine is behind the pistol grip and trigger.

improved the trigger mechanism and sights. After that, Kalashnikov applied the same mechanism to a light machine gun family, and finally, in 1974, produced a new version of the rifle in 5.45mm caliber. By that time the Soviets had licensed production to Finland, China, North Korea, Iraq, Egypt, and many other countries, and features taken from the Kalashnikov design had shown up in several other rifle designs.

But in 1947 nobody outside the Soviet Union knew anything about the AK rifle, and they were all pursuing their own ideas. For the revelation of the German Sturmgewehr and its short cartridge had caused designers in several Western countries to reach for their pencils.

Stefan Januscewski was a Polish engineer who worked in the Polish national arsenal at Radom in the 1930s. When war came he was mobilized into the army, escaped both Germans and Russians and made his way to France and then Britain, where he became one of the "Polish Design Team" at the Royal Small Arms Factory, Enfield Lock. As the war ended he began developing a new rifle just as an "Ideal Caliber Board" were deliberating over a replacement for the .303 cartridge. They, like others, reached the conclusion that 7mm was the ideal, and they developed a short 7mm cartridge of excellent ballistic properties, leaving Jansen (as he now called himself after naturalization) to develop his rifle around it. The result was the EM2 (Enfield Model 2) which broke a lot of new ground in military rifle design.

Although Jansen had never seen the Kalashnikov design there are several similarities in the EM2 which reinforce the old belief that if you give competent engineers the same problem they will often come up independently with similar answers. The EM2 used a gas cylinder above the barrel, the piston continuing back to become the bolt carrier, into the bottom of which the bolt was inserted. Locking of the bolt was not done by rotation, however, but by two symmetrical lugs at the sides of the bolt which were cammed outward to lock into recesses in the receiver body. But the most innovative feature of the rifle was the fact that the barrel

was set right back in the stock so that the rear of the action was separated from the firer's shoulder only by the butt pad and the chamber lay alongside his face. This placed the magazine behind the trigger and pistol grip and it allowed the rifle to have a full-length barrel and yet be shorter, overall, than a conventionally stocked rifle with the same barrel length. This layout is always called the "bull-pup" layout, though nobody can come up with an explanation of how this name was adopted. The only drawback to this system is that since there is no drop in the butt, to bring the rifle up in front of the firer's eye, the sights have to be set very high, and Jansen made another innovative step; he formed a carrying handle on the top of the receiver and incorporated an optical sight inside it.

The EM2 was a remarkable weapon and a highly effective one. Production was organized and as the Rifle, 7mm, No 9 Mark I it was approved for service in June 1951, and almost immediately placed on hold. There were political questions to be answered before the British Army could have a new rifle. In brief, it was a question of standardization within the newly-formed NATO organization, and the USA, in particular, was blind to the advantages of a short cartridge, insisting that it needed the full-sized .30 caliber cartridge. There was no reasoning with them, and since they carried the greatest weight in NATO their views carried the day. Paying lip-service to the short cartridge concept they cobbled up a fractionally shorter version of the .30-06 cartridge and this became the 7.62mm NATO rifle round. It proved impossible to re-design the EM2 to take this round so the rifle was abandoned. Stefan Jansen left the UK shortly afterwards and took his expertise to Canada and then to the USA, eventually becoming Director of Weapons Research for Winchester.

All of which left a tremendous gap in NATO where the British ought to have had an automatic rifle. But relief was at hand. Fabrique National de Armes de Guerre of Herstal, Belgium, was a long-established firm who had made all sorts of military weapons since the 1890s. Re-organized after the war, they had picked up on an automatic rifle design they had

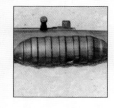

Right: A British soldier of the Green Howards Regiment with manpack radio and FN FAL rifle.

Below: Three slightly varying versions of the 7.62mm FN FAL rifle, used by over 55 countries around the world.

been developing in 1940 when they were rudely interrupted by the German Army. At the same time they had watched the progress of the NATO squabble and could see, clearer than any of the participants, what the result was going to be. So they overhauled the automatic rifle design again, and then sat waiting to see what the chosen cartridge would be. Once they knew that they simply bored out the rifle chamber to suit and sent their salesmen forth.

The resulting rifle was as big a success, in its own way, as the Kalashnikov. The FN Fusil Automatique Legere or "FAL" was eventually adopted by more than 55 countries around the world — more significantly, it was the first foreign rifle ever to become the standard weapon of the British Army. Gas-operated, it locked the breech by tilting the bolt so that it wedged into a recess in the receiver. It was designed as a selective-fire weapon although most armies chose not to have automatic fire since such fire with the 7.62 NATO cartridge rendered the weapon barely controllable unless it was on a bipod and being used as a machine gun.

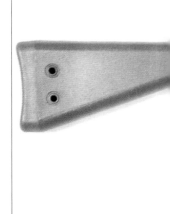

Above: British troops in chemical protective clothing with a Carl Gustav 84mm recoilless gun and their personal FN FAL rifles.

Above Right: The latest version of the German Heckler & Koch 7.62mm is this G3A3 with plastic furniture and with the safety and fire selector lever duplicated on the right side for ease of use by left-handed soldiers.

Right: A German soldier in 1985 with his G3 rifle; this is a later version with plastic furniture.

In the aftermath of the war many countries re-equipped their forces with American or British weapons that were surplus to the requirements of their original owners. Now that NATO was beginning to come together there was a need to clear these weapons away and re-equip to the new standard, and even if the country was not a member of NATO, adoption of a NATO-standard caliber or weapon was often a political statement of alignment and also a guarantee that the weapon in question was to a reputable standard and that spares and maintenance would be readily available. This led to a demand which, in many cases was met by the FN FAL rifle, but there was enough room for another major player to enter the arena.

Another feature of the immediate postwar years was the number of German designers who suddenly appeared in strange places; one group surfaced in Spain, where they became the nucleus of a government design center known as CETME (Center for Technical Studies of Military Equipment). Some of these men had been developing a new assault rifle in the Mauser factory, the Sturmgewehr 45, which had barely reached prototype stage when the war ended. They now took this as their starting point and developed a rifle using a roller-delayed blowback bolt mechanism. Two rollers on the bolt were cammed out into recesses in

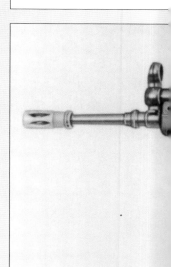

Top Right: A more specialized variant of the G3 is this MSG-90 sniping rifle. Note that there are no iron sights, and that a bipod and an adjustable butt with cheek-rest are provided.

Middle Right: The US Rifle M14 was simply a Garand with a removable 20-round box magazine instead of the original 8-round clip-loaded integral magazine. It was also in 7.62mm NATO caliber instead other the old .30-06 caliber.

Below Right: The basic G3 rifle has given rise to a wide variety of derivative models in various calibers. This is the G41A3 in 5.56mm NATO caliber and with a 30-round magazine which is interchangeable with that of the US M16 rifle.

the receiver to hold the bolt closed during firing, and these were slowly forced back into the bolt by the pressure of the fired case pushing backwards, until they were entirely free and the bolt could move. They developed a rifle for the Spanish Army and then licensed a Dutch firm to make it; the Dutch interested the newly-formed West German Army in the design. They found it a little rough in spots, especially in 7.62mm NATO caliber, and handed it to a new company called Heckler & Koch who had set up in business across the street from Mauser. Heckler & Koch had so far made only a blowback pistol but they took on the task of sanitizing the rifle design and shortly perfected a weapon which the West German Army were happy to accept as the Gewehr 3 or "G3." German acceptance gave it a guarantee of serviceability and soon the G3 was arming several other countries, from Portugal to Norway and Pakistan. Licenses to manufacture were arranged, and at the present time the G3 has seen service in about 60 countries and has been manufactured in 12.

America, having been responsible for the 7.62mm NATO cartridge, armed themselves with what was little more than an up-dated Garand — the M14 rifle. This took the original Garand and converted it to 7.62mm caliber, fitted a removable 20-round magazine, and made some other minor improvements. A sound enough weapon, an attempt to then give it automatic fire and use it as a machine gun proved disastrous. But the Americans, by that time, were preparing to make a major upheaval in the military rifle scene.

The war, followed by the Korean War in 1950–53 had more or less convinced many people in the USA that expecting soldiers to shoot straight in combat was a forlorn hope. What was needed was some weapon which would compensate for the lack of skill or for human error in aiming, and much energy and money was spent in the 1955–65 period in search of this. Cartridges holding two or three bullets were tried, the theory being that if he missed with the first bullet, then the other one or two might hit the target. Cartridges using flechettes — tiny needle-like finned darts — were tried, on the same assumption. Rifles which fired

Above: Firing the US M14 rifle.

Above Right: The original AR15/M16 rifle, recognizable by the triangular fore-end and the short muzzle with three-prong flash hider. The rear sight is in the carrying handle, which is why the foresight has to be set so high.

Right: Stripping the M16A2 to clean it is very simple; remove a locking pin and it hinges open like a shotgun, allowing the bolt and cocking handle to be withdrawn.

three fast shots for a single pull of the trigger were tried, as were many more ideas, but out of all this very little of any value appeared; some of the ideas were good, but the technology was not available to make the best of them. One thing that did become apparent was that if the cartridge was lighter than the 7.62mm NATO round, then the recoil was less and there was a better chance that the soldier might put his first shot somewhere into the target. Moreover, he might find it possible to use an automatic weapon without scattering his shots all over the landscape. And a smaller cartridge would be lighter, and permit a lighter rifle. In other words, the Americans had suddenly realized what the British and others had been trying to tell them ten years before, that a short cartridge would confer advantages, and they set about to re-invent their weaponry.

Not that any of this came from official sources. A designer by the name of Eugene Stoner had been given the task of developing a suitable 7.62mm rifle by a private company, the ArmaLite Division of Fairchild Aircraft, but soon saw the advantages of a smaller cartridge. He took an existing sporting round, the .222 Remington, and built his rifle around it. It didn't work quite as well as he wanted, so he redesigned the .222 Remington with a slightly larger cartridge case and called it the .223 Remington. His rifle worked by gas, but instead of the usual gas piston arrangement he merely piped the gas back and blew it directly against the bolt carrier. He laid out the butt in a straight line behind the receiver so as to reduce any tendency for the rifle to climb around the firer's

shoulder, which meant raising the sight line, and therefore, like Stefan Jansen, he put a carrying handle in top and fitted his sight to that, though he didn't go as far as using an optical sight. The result became the ArmaLite AR-15.

By this time the Vietnam war had begun and the US Air Force needed a rifle to supply to South Vietnamese troops guarding its airfields. The M14 was too much of a handful for these men, small of stature, and this ArmaLite weapon seemed to fill the bill. And once they were equipped with it, American soldiers looked enviously at a weapon which appeared to be about half the bulk and weight of the M14 they were carrying through the jungles. Special Forces tried it and found it good and, after a

Above: Be a rifle ever so good, there is always somebody willing to improve it. Here is the M16A1 rifle with a 90-round magazine added.

good deal of political infighting, the AR15 became the M16 and a general issue, largely replacing the M14 in Vietnam. And then, in the late 1960s, after field experience with the M16, the US Army announced that the .223 (5.56mm) M16 rifle would henceforth be the standard US Army rifle, replacing the 7.62mm M14. Which, of course, simply blew NATO standardization out of the window.

What made things worse was that everybody in NATO had outfitted themselves with 7.62mm rifles in the mid-1950s, and the life of an assault rifle was reckoned as being 25 to 30 years, by which time its repair bill would have exceeded its capital value and, in any case, a fresh generation of technology would have come along and rendered it obsolete. So nobody was looking to replace their rifles until the middle 1980s. And here were the Americans setting up a new standard without reference to anybody else.

The M16 rifle did set a new standard. It was light, accurate, and, after initial teething troubles had been rectified, reliable and robust. Moreover, it rapidly acquired a reputation for devastating effects on its targets. Exaggerated stories of the lethality of the bullet began to circulate in the 1960s — it was claimed that the bullet "tumbled in flight and caused enormous wounds," though how it managed to remain accurate if the bullet was turning over and over was never satisfactorily explained. The truth of the matter was that the combination of bullet weight, velocity, and spin rate was such that the bullet remained stable in flight but became unstable when it struck anything. It did deliver severe wounds, but, in truth, these were really no worse that the wounds delivered by heavier bullets in the past.

As a result, several smaller countries needing military rifles were happy to adopt it, and forward-looking gunmakers were soon producing designs for 5.56mm rifles. Most were simply adaptations of their existing 7.62mm

Below: The M16A2 made by Colt, has a heavy and stiff barrel NATO rifling, and a few other refinements, but the basic weapon is still that of the AR15 pattern.

Bottom: The M16A1 was the version which went into military service; it had a longer barrel and also a plunger to assist in closing the bolt if the chamber was dirty and the cartridge reluctant to go in.

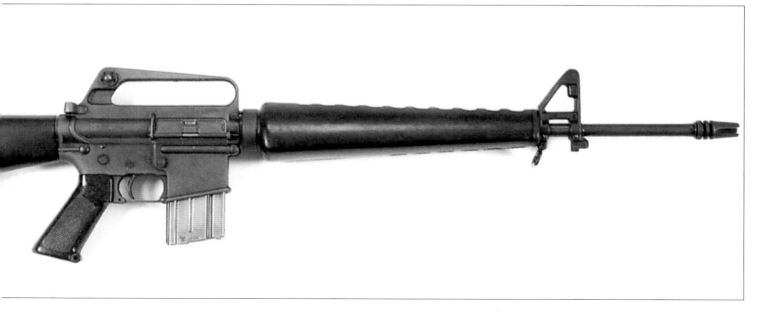

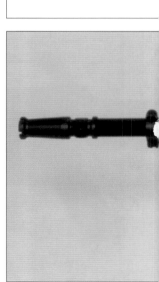

Right: The "Space Age Rifle." The Steyr-Mannlicher AUG 5.56mm assault rifle in short-barrelled form. A bullpup, with the magazine behind the trigger, the plastic housing contains all the metal parts and the carrying handle is a telescope sight. The front handle folds forward for those who prefer to hold the rifle in the traditional manner.

Below: The AUG rifle, standard length pattern with five magazines, 150 rounds of 5.56mm ammunition, and two rifle grenades which can be fired off the muzzle without requiring any special fittings.

designs, but one firm, Steyr-Mannlicher of Austria, took an enormous stride when they were asked to produce a new service rifle by the Austrian Army in the early 1970s. They developed the Armee Universal Gewehr (Army Universal Gun) which used a futuristic plastic stock into which a gas-actuated selective-fire bullpup rifle was built. Moreover, the components were "modular;" in other words the various units which went to make up the rifle — the barrel, receiver, firing mechanism — were interchangeable. So the rifle could be fitted with barrels of various lengths to make it into a carbine, a rifle, or a light machine gun. The standard receiver had a carrying handle with an optical sight, but this could be changed for one with a carrying handle formed into a flat plat-form for mounting electro-optical or other types of sight. The standard firing mechanism offered single shots or automatic fire, but could be removed and changed for one offering single shots only, or one which offered single shots or three-round bursts. The rifle could be adapted for left or right-handed firers by moving the extractor and closing or opening an ejector slot on either side of the plastic body.

The AUG was adopted by the Austrian Army in 1979 and thereafter spread across the world, eventually coming into use in the Middle East, by Australia and New Zealand, and even by the US Customs Service.

The success of the AUG stimulated interest in the 5.56mm cartridge, and between 1977 and 1980 NATO held a long and exhaustive trial to

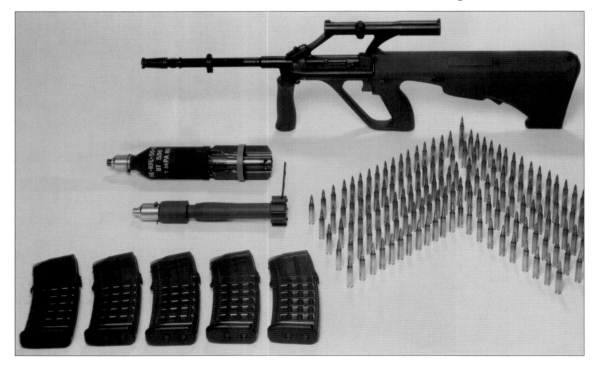

determine the standard infantry rifle caliber for the next generation of weapons. It was generally accepted that 5.56mm would be the chosen cartridge, and this turned out to be true, but with a heavier bullet than had previously been used, one which required a slower twist of rifling for stability. With the agreement on the 5.56mm as NATO standard, there was now the need to replace the rifles of NATO armies with 5.56mm weapons.

France, although not then a full member of NATO had moved first and adopted the FAMAS (Fusil Automatique, Manufacture d'Armes de Saint Etienne) in 1975. This used a delayed blowback mechanism and, again, was a bullpup design with the mechanism alongside the firer's face. Britain began work in the middle 1970s, developed a new rifle in 4.85mm caliber which was theoretically superior to the 5.56mm from the ballistic point of view, but the designers had sufficient sense to realize there was little chance of this becoming NATO standard and had designed the rifle so that a redesign to 5.56mm caliber was feasible. This duly took place and in 1985 the SA80 (Small Arm for the '80s) appeared. Another

Above: Another view of the CETME Model L 5.56mm rifle, this time in the hands of a Spanish soldier. The forward cocking handle, just by his forward hand, indicates the same system of operation as that of the G3 rifle.

Right: A member of the Spanish police anti-terrorist squad demonstrates the CETME 5.56mm Model L rifle, a weapon using much the same mechanism as the German G3.

bullpup, gas operated, and with an optical sight, it promised a great deal, but due to the closure of the Royal Small Arms Factory at the crucial time of moving from development to production, quality control went to pieces and the first rifles to go into service were faulty. This, of course, is nothing new; very few rifles have ever been a complete success from the very beginning, but the SA80 became something of a political football before the defects were corrected; as Josh Billings, the American philosopher, once said "A reputation once broken may possibly be repaired, but the world will always keep their eyes on the spot where the crack was."

But the most remarkable weapon to appear at the NATO trial was a German rifle, the Heckler & Koch G11. In 1970, the German Army had asked for a selective fire rifle with a very high probability of hitting with the first round, and they suggested that this might be obtained by firing a controlled three-round burst. Several other people have done the same thing, but H&K looked rather more closely into this proposal and saw the fundamental drawback: firing such a burst means that the first round goes where the soldier aims it; the second is fired as the rifle is recoiling from

Above: The French FAMAS G-1 5.56mm rifle was the first bullpup to actually get into the hands of troops, when the French Army adopted it. A delayed blowback weapon, its iron sights are concealed in the top of the long carrying handle.

Right: The FAMAS is so compact that it has entirely replaced the sub-machine gun in the French Army and is gradually doing so in the French police as well. Here is a mounted Gendarme with a black FAMAS slung across his shoulder.

the first shot and therefore goes rather higher; and the third is fired as the rifle is recoiling even more, having added the impulse of the second shot to the rising barrel due to the first shot, so that the third shot never goes anywhere near the target. Mathematical and physical considerations indicated that the three rounds had to be fired at a rate of about 2,000 rounds per minute to land reasonably close together, and this was impossible with the conventional rifle mechanism.

Seeking a solution to this insoluble problem, H&K decided to adopt a new type of cartridge, a caseless cartridge, one on which there was no conventional brass or steel cartridge case. Instead, the cartridge was a block of solid propellant into which a bullet was embedded at one end and a combustible percussion cap at the other. The advantage of this was that once the round was fired, there was nothing left inside the rifle, and therefore nothing to extract and eject. A major part of the operating cycle of the normal rifle had been removed. Without the need to eject, fresh rounds could be loaded in more rapidly. Of course, it was hardly as simple as that. In the first place, the metal cartridge case also acts as a seal to prevent propellant gas leaking out across the bolt; it also acts as a heat barrier between the hot chamber walls and the sensitive propellant powder. So the breech mechanism of the rifle had to be completely new, as did the propellant powder.

The eventual G11 rifle, as it appeared for the NATO trials, used a rotating breech-block with a magazine feeding into it from above, dropping the cartridge into the block nose-first. The block then turned through 90 degrees and the cap was fired by a firing pin, sending the bullet up the barrel. How the breech was sealed is something which has never been publicly explained, remaining a secret, but a German officer who was involved with the trial once said that it resembled the Wankel engine in

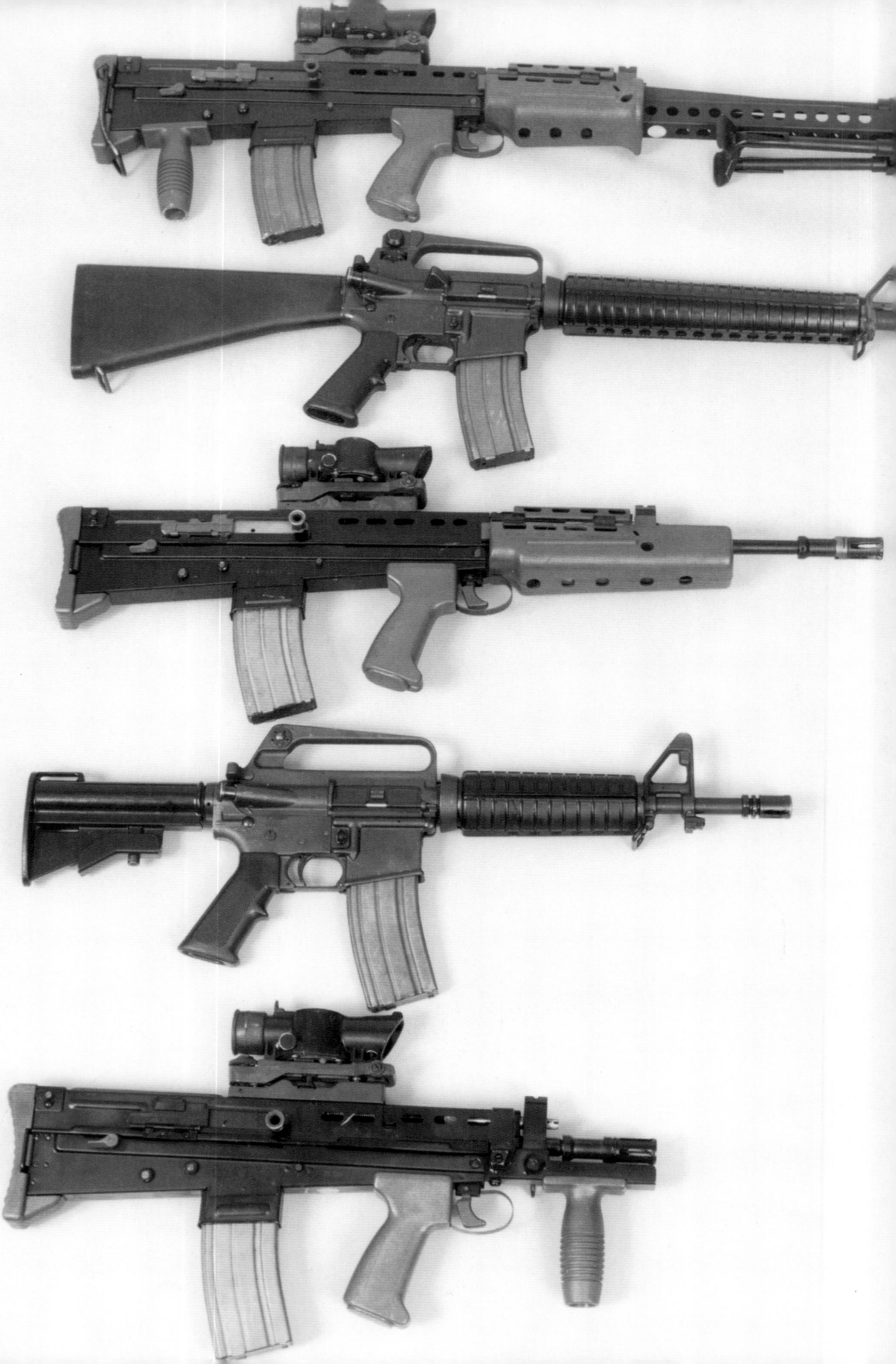

his Audi, which suggests the use of seals around the edge of the breech block. This action takes place at single shot or automatic fire. But when the three-round burst is selected, some very strange things take place.

The mechanism of the rifle floats freely inside a plastic outer casing. On firing the first shot of the three-round burst the mechanism begins to recoil in the casing. As it does so the rifle is reloaded and fires the second shot; this merely adds to the recoil movement, and the third shot is loaded and fired. Then, and only then, is the recoil movement completed and only then does the firer feel the recoil and the rifle begin to rise as it pivots against his shoulder. The three rounds have left the gun at a rate of 2,100 rounds per minute — the impression on the firer is of a prolonged explosion rather than three distinct reports — before the recoil is able to move the barrel upwards and all three bullets land within about a foot of each other at 200 meters range.

The G11 was withdrawn from the trials due to problems with its propellant, but those were cleared up and the German Army committed itself to adoption of this new rifle, in 4.7mm caliber, in 1980. But in 1988 the Berlin Wall came down — East Germany was re-united with West Germany, the West German economy had to be milked to fund revival of the East, and, of course, the first source to be plundered was the defence budget. After the Army had received about 1,000 rifles for the Special Forces, the government cancelled the contract and that was the

Above: The British Army's SA80 5.56mm rifle, complete with optical sight. Another bullpup, to obtain the desired length of barrel inside a short all-over length, this originated as a 4.85mm weapon but was changed to conform with the new NATO cartridge standard.

Left: Comparisons — from the top, the SA80 light machine gun, the US M16A1 rifle, SA80 infantry rifle, US M16A2 Commando carbine, SA80 carbine. The SA80 carbine has not been issued.

Above: The futuristic Heckler and Koch G11 rifle which fires caseless cartridges. The magazine lies along the top of the barrel and feeds downward. The rotary handle on the side, behind the pistol grip, is operated to load and unload the chamber. This rifle was issued to German Special Forces in 1990.

Below: British Royal Marine Commandos and their SA80 weapons; the right-hand man in the back row holds the light machine gun version, the remainder the rifle

end of the G11 rifle. It was almost the end of Heckler & Koch, but they were rescued by British Aerospace.

The G11 made a reappearance in the early 1990s in the course of the American Advanced Combat Rifle program. This was a study set up by the US Army to see what sort of technology could be applied to the next generation of infantry rifles due in the closing years of the century. They originally asked for a caseless solution, to which Heckler & Koch responded, and then expanded the program by inviting other manufacturers to submit any ideas they wanted; the sole stipulation was that their rifle had to show a considerably increased hit probability over the existing M16A1 rifle. Of a variety of weapons suggested by various makers, four were selected to be manufactured and tested; one was the G11; one was a design by Steyr-Mannlicher using a plastic cartridge case and firing flechettes; one was by Colt, an improved M16 firing a double-bullet cartridge; and the fourth was by the AAI corporation, also firing flechettes. All worked well, but none of them managed to improve the hit probability by the necessary degree and the program was concluded with no rifle being selected for further development.

Above Left: The Heckler & Koch Advanced Combat Rifle for the USA was based on the G11 but had some slight differences in layout and appearance. The lip around the end of the barrel casing stops the careless hand slipping in front of the muzzle, and the magazine (black) is easily visible above the casing.

Below Left: Steyr-Mannlicher's entry for the Advanced Combat Rifle contest. It used a plastic casing like the AUG and was also a bullpup. Note the shotgun-style aiming rib above the barrel as an aid to quick snap-shooting.

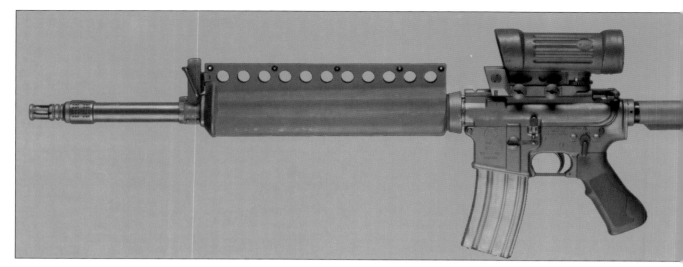

Top: The Colt Advance Combat Rifle was obviously a descendant of the M16 and, indeed, used many components of that rifle. But it was designed to fire a special cartridge with two bullets to improve the chance of hitting.

Above: The Advanced Combat Rifle designed by the AAI Corporation used a conventional layout but had what resembled half a revolver cylinder inside it, which flipped across and presented three rounds to the barrel in very rapid succession to get a very fast three-round burst.

This trial cost the US taxpayer something in the order of $350 million, and it reinforced a belief which had been hardening among small arms experts for some time. That the development of the rifle has now reached a point where any technological advance is going to be very difficult, very expensive, and probably not worth either the effort or the money expended. The rifle, as it stands today, is efficient, has greater accuracy than the average soldier is capable of using, is lethal, and is cost-effective. This goes for commercial rifles as well as military rifles. A century and a half of development of the breech-loading, central-fire cartridge rifle has brought it to a point of perfection where significant improvement in reliability or accuracy is almost impossible. Some manufacturing improvements may be possible; it may be feasible to make barrels of ceramic material which will resist wear better than steel — we don't really know, and several years of experimentation lie ahead before we will have the answer. It may be possible to make subtle improvements to bullets to improve their accuracy and target effect. It may be possible to improve propellant chemistry to generate more velocity and hence slightly improve accuracy by reducing the time of flight. But all of these will cost large sums of money in experiments, and the open question is whether the improvement so gained — an extra few hundred feet per second of velocity, an extra 5,000 rounds through a barrel before it loses accuracy — will, in real life, be of sufficient value to make the expenditure worth while. We shall just have to wait and see.

  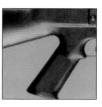

Below: Firing the Swiss Army's standard Sturmgewehr 90 rifle.

References

Gun related internet sites

There is a wealth of information available on the internet about guns and rifles, the following is an introduction to some of the more interesting ones. These sites are liable to change but these should provide a good starting point.

The Old Western Scrounger has limited edition, antique and collector's items. A "niche" company that specializes in hard-to-get ammunition from all over the world. There is also a custom loading service that can provide ammunition to fit virtually all calibers of obsolete weapons or create from scratch:
http://www.snowcrest.net/oldwest/index2.html

The Federal Hunt Club, features an ammunition catalog, interactive tools, museum, gear and Shooting Resource Center. The STSS (Support The Shooting Sports) Program focuses on initiatives that directly affect the environment and future of shooting and hunting while helping youngsters learn about conservation.
http://www.federalcartridge.com/

The web site of Master Gunsmith Andreas Baumkircher. handguns featured include the Billinghurst Underhammer Caplock, the Calderwood Underhammer Flintlock and Adams Revolver. rifles featured are the Billinghurst Overhammer Caplock and Flintlock Rifle:
http://www.baumkircher.com/page3.html

Ace Custom 45's Inc (located in Texas) the home of the 45 SUPER. Specializing in converting Colt style 1911 pistols and Smith and Wesson models into 45 SUPERs. Also offered is a complete custom gunsmithing service:
http://www.acecustom45.com

The Parris Manufacturing Company. At the start of World War II when there were no rifles available for training purposes, the Parris Manufacturing Company was asked by the Department of Defence to make over two-million dummy training rifles for the Army and Navy. The company now specialises in replicas of every rifle, musket or pistol that played an important part in American history:
http://www.parrismfg.com

Created for collectors of Colt Automatic Pistols, specifically for the Colt Pocket Hammerless Models. The site includes general, and in some cases, specific information on most pre-World War II Colt Automatic Models, with serial number, date of product, disassembly instructions and parts diagrams:

http://www.coltautos.com

An informative site from MoveOn.Org containing a compiled petition fon gun safety legislation. Gives detailed information on the impact of firearms in modern-day society:

http://www.moveon.org/children/index.html

Books on guns —— references & bibliography

Baderson, Robert H; **The Official Guide to Gunmarks**; House of Collectibles, 1996. Identifies manufacturer marks that appear on American and foreign pistols, rifles and shotguns. Good reference for the discerning collector who visits gunshows and auctions. The book offers professional advice, helping collectors to spot valuable rarities as well as fakes and forgeries. A special section translates the Waffenamt numerical system, used by the Germans during WWII in lieu of manufacturer names.

Cooper, Jeff; **The Art of the Rifle**; Paladin Press; 1997. This book, written by a firearms expert, makes excellent reading for the sports person.

Malloy, John; **Complete Guide to Guns and Shooting**; Dbi Books, 1995. This book covers all the basics of guns and shooting. The information is mostly introductory but would benefit the experienced shooter as well.

McDowell, Bruce, A.; **A Study of Colt Conversions and Other Percussion Revolvers**; Krause Publications, 1997. A study of various models of cartridge conversion revolvers including details on how many guns were produced and any variations during production.

Pate, Charles W.; US **Handguns of World War II**: The Secondary Pistols and Revolvers; Andrew Mowbray Publishing, 1998. Pate, a retired US military officer and respected authority on military weapons, focuses his attention on the lesser known pistols and revolvers — both commercial and military — used during the war.

Taffin, John; **Big Bore Sixguns**; Krause Publications, 1997. A well illustrated and researched book on sixguns, particularly the single action revolver. Detailed information on guns, cartridges, and reloads.

Traister, John E.; **Antique Guns: The Collectors Guide**; Stoeger Publishing Company, 1994. This book covers a vast spectrum of pre-1900 firearms manufactured by U.S gunmakers, Canadian, French, German, Belgium and Spanish companies. Offers detailed descriptions, production dates, and current values.

Zhuk, A.B., Walters, John, eds.; **The Illustrated Encyclopedia of Handguns: Pistols and Revolvers of the World, 1870 to the present**; Greenhill Military Paperbacks, 1997. Includes a vast collection of sketches and illustrations of thousands of handguns from around the world and across time. It is organized by countries of manufacture and includes briefs on the companies references.

Credits

The photography for this book comes from the collection of the author, Ian Hogg. Both he and the publisher wish to gratefully acknowledge the assistance of all the manufacturers who generously contributed photographs. They include:

Armalon, UK
Armi Beretta, Italy
Barrett Firearms, USA
Ceska Zbrojovka, Czech Republic
CETME, Spain
Famae, Chile
FN Herstal, Belgium
Franchi SpA, Itlay
Glat, France
Glick Ges mbH, Austria
Harris Firearms, USA
Heckler and Koch GmbH, Germany
Israel Military Industries, Israel
Mauser-Werke, Germany
Musgrave, South Africa
SIG, Switzerland
Socimi, SpA, Italy
Sphinx Engineering, Switzerland
Steyr Mannlicher GmbH, Austria
Fra. Tanfoglio, Italy